JUST PLAIN BILL

Here, There & Everywhere

A Clarification of Reality

BALBOA PRESS

A DIVISION OF HAY HOUSE

Balboa Press books may be ordered through booksellers or by contacting:

Balboa Press
A Division of Hay House
1663 Liberty Drive
Bloomington, IN 47403
www.balboapress.com
1 (877) 407-4847

Because of the dynamic nature of the Internet, any web addresses or links contained in this book may have changed since publication and may no longer be valid. The views expressed in this work are solely those of the author and do not necessarily reflect the views of the publisher, and the publisher hereby disclaims any responsibility for them.

The author of this book does not dispense medical advice or prescribe the use of any technique as a form of treatment for physical, emotional, or medical problems without the advice of a physician, either directly or indirectly. The intent of the author is only to offer information of a general nature to help you in your quest for emotional and spiritual well-being. In the event you use any of the information in this book for yourself, which is your constitutional right, the author and the publisher assume no responsibility for your actions.

Any people depicted in stock imagery provided by Getty Images are models, and such images are being used for illustrative purposes only.
Certain stock imagery © Getty Images.

Printed in the United States of America.

ISBN: 978-1-9822-0239-2 (sc)
ISBN: 978-1-9822-0241-5 (hc)
ISBN: 978-1-9822-0240-8 (e)

Library of Congress Control Number: 2018904614

Balboa Press rev. date: 04/24/2018

Contents

Acknowledgments ix
Who Is Just Plain Bill? 1
It Begins 3
The Secret of Everywhere 5
We Are All Connected 7
A Child Returns 9
Grains of Sand 12
Balance 15
A Basket of Lessons 18
Close Calls 21
Lamar the Philosopher 24
Cloaks 28
Values and the Wave 31
Continued Learning 35
Vacation 39
Fredericko's Gang Life 43
Distractions 47
Tabitha's Short Journey 51
Peggy the Parrot 54
Being Twins 58
Passing and Returning 62
The Spark 65
Bad Dreams 69
Renauld the Painter 72
Moving Forward 75
Global Warming and Mother Nature 78
Chernobyl 81

Gossip with Abby..84

Journeys...87

Annie … Finding the Soul...90

Planetary Travel...94

What's in a Name?..98

Why Fear?...103

Sudden Uncloaking..107

Making Decisions...112

Bunny and Hunter...116

Jake's Deer Company...120

Never Give Up..125

Everyone Has Talent...130

Festival of the Catch...134

Spot...138

Learning from Nature...143

Warrior of the Wind...147

The Secret to Success..151

The Cave...155

Pap's Reminder...160

Taking the Fork in the Road..164

McGee Gets His Stripes..169

Andy … Tradition and Values..174

The Neighbor's Farm..178

Understanding the Wave...184

The Quality of Goodness..190

Pap's Message..195

It is with great love and pride that I dedicate this effort to my Nana and Pap, Helen and Ervin Holtry. They lived their lives honoring life and family by setting an example of how, during our journeys, we are here to learn lessons and, in many cases, create examples to last a lifetime.

My Nana and Pap did just that. They didn't worry about themselves but only about others. Whether a close relative, a neighbor, or a friend, everyone felt special having the experience of knowing two wonderful people who knew only of caring and loving others. They did so quietly and with no fanfare. It was just the right thing to do, as they would often say.

I miss my Nana and Pap tremendously. But I also know that all who crossed paths with them feel the same. So, Pap and Nana, this book is dedicated to you. Thank you for just being you and sharing the simplicity of life with us all.

Acknowledgments

Special thanks to my dear wife, Susan, whose love, support, and hard work provided the ability to grasp and understand the gift I have received to be able to write this book. Without Susie, I know I could never have been able to live the life of being Just Plain Bill. Thank you to my sweetheart for your hard work and understanding.

I love you so.

Who Is Just Plain Bill?

I was born on March 27, 1948, to a farm family in central Pennsylvania. Our family always identified ourselves as just Plain People, somewhere in between Mennonites and Amish. When I was young, I remember looking up Plain People in the encyclopedia, and frankly, it accurately described my family. We were a typical large farm family, as we lived with my grandparents, aunts, and uncles.

My pony, Nellie, and I were born on the same day. From day one, we had a special bond as we grew up together. She was my favorite, along with our collie, Major. Each of us thought Major was our protector from the outside world, or at least I thought so.

Being the firstborn of my generation, I was the elder, like my grandfather was in our church. My father, the middle son, had to seek employment, as there were not enough assets to start a farm for him. So, my grandfather, Pap, designated me his sidekick as I was growing up on the farm. I was with Pap constantly, especially while my dad was away at the feed mill working. Our family conversations often went late into the evenings after a day in the fields.

We had many conversations on our wraparound front porch as we listened to the corn grow during summer rains. It's one of my favorite memories with my family and Pap. Pap's assignment, or at least part of it, was to prepare me for later in life when I would receive lessons from the Everywhere.

The Everywhere was something I sensed as a youngster, based on conversations with my Pap. Years later, I have learned that a great plan was created for me along the way.

In preparation, I was the first in my family to graduate from college, while little did I know what life would bring me years later. There was a grand plan, yet I was unaware.

Well into my sixty-eighth year on my current journey, I was blessed with the gift to connect with those in the Everywhere, who could tell me of great lessons learned while on their journeys and what makes the Everywhere, well, everywhere.

My Pap, as you will see, taught me well in preparation of who I was to be. Pap spent endless hours with me just being my grandpa. But even with his passing, Pap's time with me was far from finished. In fact, the lessons continue many years after his passing.

As you read, you will discover these lessons are offered for all to learn; listen and feel the values of life. These are messages that the Everywhere has prepared for us.

I am Just Plain Bill and am only the messenger. I just deliver the mail, as they say.

My hope is that you gain understanding and peace from the lessons. Make sure you focus on the true meaning of life and what it's all about for us as humans.

Always remember the values ... family, love, honor, trust, and peace. Carry these with you throughout your journey.

May you have a wonderful and peace-filled day.

It Begins

On September 12, 2016, life took an interesting turn. It was 5:15 a.m. Apparently, I had been preparing for this for a long time. It was the day after I met with a friend who is intuitively gifted. I poured my coffee, turned up the heat, and put on my blue hoodie.

As I sat down with my laptop, I opened a new document and waited. *Why am I doing this? I don't know.* Then thoughts started pouring in, and I began to type. Some call it automatic writing.

I sense the glow of spirits as they come to me. It's so natural to feel. I cannot picture their bodies, for in the Everywhere, there is no body needed.

It's like standing in a field of flowers. Every flower has its own beauty and individuality. This is how the Everywhere can best be described today. I know Everywhere will come to me differently every day, and it is always perfect.

My desire is to share what I am given in the hope that it will make a difference. I saw orbs this morning. Initially, I didn't identify them as anyone or anything specifically.

I am given that the Everywhere is a place where love, family, honor, trust, and peace prevail. There is no strife or sadness. Love is all there is. Some call it the other side, heaven, or through the veil.

These beautiful orbs are encircling me as they come down the mountain to welcome me. I recognized the energies of Pap, Nana, and many close friends. My wife who passed, Barb, is here, and although she did not spend much time in this moment with me, it was warm and complete. We accomplished our assignment. I am so happy I stayed with Barb until she passed, and she was glad I was there. We completed our assignment.

My grandfather, Pap, has always been there for me. His guidance is so loving and wonderful. I honor his presence in watching over me when he was here in human form and now as he stays with me in spirit. And Nana, my grandmother whom everyone adored, is always supporting and loving even though not usually communicating with me. Just her presence in my heart is so perfect.

The lessons are here. Feeling the love of the orbs is such an overwhelming gift. I cannot see details, only presences in the orbs. It is a feeling of purpose and completion as I travel among them to gather information. Those in the Everywhere are here to help, guide, and support all of us on our journey.

The Everywhere is like a waterless ocean of *all that is*. In our current lives, we are part of the whole. Lives now, before, and after sort of happen concurrently, although the only life we currently sense is our present life, which we refer to "life as we know it." It is life as we know it *now*, but the real life we comprehend is always, ever present, and our soul is a part of the whole.

Each of us has meaning and values to learn before we move on.

Value is life.

Every living thing is important. There are no differences here. Differences exist only in our minds. We are teased with the temptation of trying to be different, and yet we really are not.

We are an ever-evolving, individual presence that is always learning new lessons to continue to keep our souls living in the moment.

So, really, death is a state of mind. Our presence continues in our spirit. It is like hanging up our robe (our body) and stepping as spirit into the Everywhere.

When we say, "the power and the glory of the soul," this is the true meaning of everywhere and everything. The power and the glory of the spirit. It is the true meaning of life. The power of it *all*.

This is special. I sense the orbs represent so many thousands and thousands around me who are smiling and saying ... "Yeah, it's okay."

It's all about love and happiness.

Be a good spirit ...

Be in good spirits ...

That's all for today ...

The Secret of Everywhere

What is interesting to me this morning is the feeling of family. Most of my ancestors, if not all, came from somewhere in Europe, primarily in the Germany/Netherlands area. I think my Nana's family came from England or Wales. Many have a great desire to learn of their heritage. It is my understanding that eight brothers named Holtry came over in the late 1700s and landed in Philadelphia to settle in the Reading, Pennsylvania, area, at least for a bit of time. And then some ventured farther west as far as 120 miles.

There are many families with similar beginnings in the United States, whose heritage traces back to Europe and beyond. We all refer to them as our past. Some use the term *blood relatives*, and even though this may be true, it's the humanly way of tracking our past. It's all about tracking back in time as best as we can to try to decipher our origins. I guess you could say the same for trees, birds, fish, bears, lions, and all of nature. All parts of nature came from its heritage, part of the great design of Mother Nature.

It feels as if Pap says, "And that's the end of the story." At least for the earthly Mother Nature story. But as I am learning, our past heritage is our way of trying to piece together an understanding. What or who is Mother Nature, especially knowing that our bodies are only vessels/cloaks of this journey?

Are the vessels/cloaks the true mystery of what we try to learn and understand? And in reality, the Everywhere creates this and other dimensions to share their own stories and journeys. When in fact the Everywhere knowingly shares that each of us in the Everywhere is from Everywhere. Our journeys, assigned as they are, go to journeys of Everywhere all the time.

The secret of Everywhere is organizing our feelings and thoughts to maintain some type of normalcy and learning from each journey.

The full understanding of the reality of Everywhere is between journeys when we all connect in purity and peace. You can feel the presence while returning to the Everywhere. It does not matter about our journeys. Some senses of déjà vu occur from time to time for us all, but the Everywhere is a grand understanding of the trivialness of it all, when we gather in the Everywhere.

Pure joy, happiness, love, and the sense of belonging in the Everywhere. Journeys are short in time and are just a smidgeon of the grand existence of the Everywhere. It's like a speck of dust in the grand plan, as time as we know it does not exist in the Everywhere.

There are millions of planets. Imagine the true hugeness of Everywhere. We sense the grand Everywhere in this dimension as we reach out to learn about our existence on earth, only to see the endless number of dimensions existing simultaneously.

And yet we continue to try to piece together a worldly understanding of our grand picture here on earth. Every journey is important to us, as we bring back lessons from each dimension to the Everywhere to share and understand.

My Pap comes to me now to assure me that I am finally understanding the Everywhere and the spirit. Pap is like a project manager for me. He continues to provide master guidance to me and others. He is a leader of sorts and coordinates my lessons to the Everywhere just like my journey here on earth. The beauty of understanding Everywhere is that every person on this earth has their own Pap who leads us Here, There, and Everywhere. Yes, everyone has a Pap, and Pap has a Pap, because Everywhere is all-knowing and all things to everyone Everywhere.

The perfection of it all is the ultimate connection.

Now it's clear to understand the presences of everyone pouring in over the mountains in the distance. As far as I can see, hundreds, thousands pouring down the mountains to me, surrounded by green and antique white orbs.

It's so beautiful.

Why, it's so Everywhere!

Love to all.

We Are All Connected

I am at "the stump" this morning. Although the wind is barely recognizable, I can sense autumn is at work. I can hear the leaves becoming more brittle as they crunch, changing from green to fall colors. But even though the calmness exists, there is activity all around me. It's as if a large doorway to the Everywhere has opened and there are spirits of beings just floating in time Everywhere, as if it is a secret time to visit the earth as we know it.

For some, it is like stepping out of the past into the present. They enjoy a basic walk in this dimension, where they can visit the Everywhere as a reminder of a past journey. I suspect this goes on a lot, as spirits have stumps in all dimensions and can visit through stumps any time they wish.

The beauty of the Everywhere is there are no rules or restrictions, only freedom to be and freedom to love one another, with no traditions or rules from a specific journey. I sense it's fun for the spirits to visit since they do not have to bring baggage with them of a current culture of a specific journey. They can just freely roam in this dimension as if not being seen by most. But those who are blessed like me can see because we understand and are not afraid but welcoming of the spirits.

We have been given the gift of understanding. Sometimes it is awkward to gather all this information because it is so overwhelming at times, but in the true moment of the moment, when a connection is being made, all that is felt is a message and the love that surrounds it. The beauty of the message is just that. It is a message with no rules or lessons. It is just a message to connect and communicate as friends, relatives, or journeys of the past. When I say journeys of the past, it is not necessarily a journey of the past. It is simply a journey because there is no time element in the Everywhere.

The old saying "what goes around, comes around" best explains the Everywhere. You really must get your arms around the messages from spirits because it must be understood that it is a message to communicate, purely and simply. It is like déjà vu all over again, as Yogi Berra would say. After all, Yogi's beautiful sayings were part of his journey. And he can visit anyone, anytime he wishes to visit from the Everywhere. Do you know why? Because he can … it's that simple. It's the beauty of the Everywhere.

Although everyone has the ability to connect with the Everywhere in their own way, many have a gift or blessing to easily connect. For some, it can take a lifetime to begin this experience. For others, it is a sporadic connection, and for some it occurs from birth. It took me sixty-eight years to understand my gift of bringing messages from the Everywhere. I don't make these up. I am the messenger, and they come to me as I type. It's as if my fingers are controlled at the time of the message. When I sit down with my laptop, I have no idea what is going to be said, and it still amazes me.

Who is to say for sure that a thought in our minds is not a visit from someone from the Everywhere? Now there is a mind bender. But hey, we are so connected to the Everywhere, can we say, for sure, that it's not that way? After all, this concept certainly didn't come from me but from the message I am receiving.

Pap is smiling and enjoying the moment because he knows how truly connected we are. We can only try to understand the unseen connection that teases us with lessons while on our journeys. Some may have a better understanding, but be assured, everyone on their journey is connected.

After all, those in the Everywhere are there only until the next journey. Then, for a fleeting moment, they are on a new journey and then back again to the Everywhere.

After all, my sixty-eight years are an element of time that only exists here and not in the Everywhere. My sixty-eight years are a snap of the finger compared to the time I have in the Everywhere.

And yes, we *all* return to the Everywhere, where the true sense of love, purity, and peace to all really exists.

Thanks, Pap, for the great morning of learning.

You have and will always bless me. I love you all.

Thanks and peace …

A Child Returns

I have been preparing for this experience for so long now. As I visit the Everywhere, I can see so many now, all warmly moving along by the hundreds. I am waiting for a spirit to visit, and then Gabby, our cat, comes up to me and tries to sit on my lap as I type. I got the message, as if she was trying to say, "Hey! what about me?" After all, she knows I have, in the past, not been a cat person and have always favored dogs, but Gabby has taught me many lessons.

Cats and all living things are part of the Everywhere, interwoven into the cast of the all-knowing and all-loving. Gabby sure does connect with me like my dog, Major, and my pony, Nellie. And as I eluded to before, my dog and my pony and my cat are not mine to own but ours to love as if family, because they are family.

Now that I have acknowledged this, Gabby has calmly sat next to me as if guarding me while I visit and learn. At the same time, I notice Pap is here to say hello with a good-morning smile. It's always so great to be in the know with Pap.

He reaches out, and as a little girl walks by, he takes her hand and brings her to meet me. She is all smiles with tight blond curls and blue-green eyes. And full of love. She just returned from a journey where although shortened in our terms of a journey, she was able to teach many of the love of family and the peace of life. She passed unexpectedly, and her family was devastated, as many are when they lose a child. But the parents, who really blessed her with a good but short journey, were so thankful to have their daughter even for a short time. They were able to understand their gift of having her with them, and they made sure all around them knew of how blessed they were for having had her in their lives.

Many people were saddened, but they were able to teach many of the love that even a short journey creates and to continue the memory of this wonderful little girl, so many could move forward in their journeys knowing they too were blessed.

It as a calming, a knowing, finally, for many. Her journey, although short, was full of memories, all good, for so many. Even more were able to learn this and move forward with a better understanding of the Everywhere. Many in this world don't truly grasp it all, as we know, but every little bit, every little morsel of love is so precious to learn. This little girl was able to do that for so many.

Was her journey so short as not to be complete? Not at all. She was able to pass a lesson to so many, as if her journey was meant to be just that. Her journey here was full and complete. And like many others who, to us here, seem to have their lives cut short for all the obvious reasons, it is their journey to be as long as it was.

The journey is over, and they return to the Everywhere, full of life, love, and the purity of peace. They are happy as always in the Everywhere, and they know their next journey will be another wonderful lesson of the Everywhere. So they return with great anticipation of continued love. It's not important that I learn the name of the little girl or her parents. It's not important that I learn any details other than what I have received. It's only important that I feel the completeness of the journey and the happiness of the little girl.

It was not a sad journey at all. All journeys are wonderful. All journeys are full of lessons, knowing a return to the Everywhere is the end of that specific journey. It's like looking forward to the next life in the Everywhere, which leads to the next journey. All is perfect. Living a journey with this understanding takes all the fear of the unknown away.

What will be will be. It's all part of the Everywhere. How beautiful this is to know. Wow.

Thank you, little girl with the beautiful, blond, curly locks. You are a joy to meet and love. Be off to your next journey. May it be as wonderful as your last. Thanks, Pap, for bringing this little bit of joy to me. I truly am blessed by her presence.

It's a great day in my journey, as Pap creates another space in my learning. Until another meeting. See you later, Pap. Have a good day.

Upward and onward, as I have said for years.

Now upward and onward rings a new ring for me. No wonder I have always said that.

Peace to all. Love …

Grains of Sand

The question of the day is, are the religions here a ruse? The answer I immediately get is "not really." Just a fearful try at the reality.

All religions, for the most part, are based on the belief that there is a single god or being that has provided the "word" to learn and worship by. In a sense, they are trying to humanize the word by giving it a timely presence, and the writings are provided by earthly teachings from a point in time designated by its "beginning."

Philosophers have taken their appropriate opportunities on their journeys to try to create a level of understanding that humans could gather around and become a group to study and worship. When that happens, a religion is created and gathers more followers over time.

It's not a bad thing to have a belief in a certain faith or religion. It is, after all, an interpretation of those disciples who rally around and create an understanding. For many, the earthly interpretation is important for an individual to understand the value of family and love. They must have a point in history in which to revere and worship.

The simplicity of a teaching started on this earth is sort of an immature version of the true reality of the Everywhere. But it is humanistic to gather around and create a family of ideas. Unfortunately, it's only a stab at the truth, as I am learning.

Religion is based on a person sent here by God to teach lessons. That in itself, if you really step back and review the concept of an earthly religion, is a veiled attempt at the truth. And for some religions, it was a form of power orated or written to create a governance over time for followers to be attracted to. Religion was not necessarily meant for wealth and power but rather to look at similar ideas to confirm an idea a person thought to hold the truth.

All religions are a personal attempt to create an understanding of life here on earth and the teachings needed to exist spiritually. So it is a natural phenomenon, so to speak. Even the lack of religion is a belief in itself.

But for those who wish to find the truth, the secrets and the answers are all around them. Can any religion explain ghosts? Not really. They sort of fear the obvious. I know ghosts are just spirits peeking through from another dimension or are caught in between.

Ghosts are in a natural process of going from the Everywhere to a new journey or coming from a journey not yet completed. That is not too difficult to understand when the Everywhere is finally realized. Neither are aliens. In fact, what I have learned so far makes so much sense. All religions seem to speak of "spirits" in some way or another. It's an attempt to get the truth. And yet the Everywhere is not hiding from the reality of the answers for anyone. As I am learning, the Everywhere is blatantly all around.

The old saying, you can't see the forest for the trees, comes to mind. And of course, déjà vu all over again is another Yogism. And I thought Yogi was just a jokester. And yes, he was a kind and loving person who, behind his celebrity, was a great man honoring his fellow persons and teaching only love and peace to all.

It's important, as it comes to me from the Everywhere, that I must not denounce religion in my teachings. It's okay to have religion, because if you do, you are actively trying to find the answers. Unfortunately, it's just a piece of the whole picture interpreted to earthly surroundings. But it's still an attempt, and that is good. Keeping the understanding of the Everywhere is to accept and add the truth of the Everywhere to the local beliefs of the times. After all, they are just bits and pieces of the true lesson of the Everywhere.

I am here to quietly bring the full understanding of the Everywhere to assist some to be more aware of their true surroundings and the understanding of each lesson here on each journey. After all, journeys are in all directions in all dimensions.

Over time, the journeys and the lessons learned will be realized more and more. The overall goal of the Everywhere it to finally reach the understanding of all journeys in all dimensions, to finally learn the complete truth.

Remember, each journey is a grain of sand, and the beach is endless. Imagine the monumental task of the Everywhere to fully teach through all the grains of sand. And yet, over eons of journeys, the full value of the Everywhere will be realized.

Peace to all as we continue on this wonderful journey to share and love. And teach …

Balance

Balance … that word—or value, as I am told—keeps coming back to me.

To most of us, balance is a word that means to equate or a leveling of sorts. Yet I am told balance is nature's way of learning. We are surrounded by balance, as I have been told. Everywhere we turn, we see balance. Day and night seem to be wrapped around the sun. In a way, it is, but balance also provides time each day for rest and work. We use a day in our lives to earn and then relax and energize by resting. Our bodies/vessels need this for balance in a day.

Summer is a time of growing and harvesting food in its simplest form, to gather supplies and such for winter as the growing season shifts to another hemisphere for its growing season.

Spring begins the new growing season and activates dormant plants to begin growing again.

Fall is the shedding or end of the growing season, preparing for the change. Yes, there are areas where seasons only adjust slightly. The seasons may not seem like they exist there, but sometimes we forget that the lack of balance in these areas shows extreme lack of seasons by definition. When I refer to lack of seasons, for example, deserts, there are areas like Central America where the oceans bring an abundance of rain from condensation. The balance of deserts are jungles, where uncontrolled growth exists because of excessive rain. And where there are jungles, nature has a way of balancing by cleaning the environment like a giant filter. The air is purified, and the water is purified. The balance of nature is at work constantly.

I just asked about climate change. Is it real or just a cycle? What is given to me is "balance." If you take away nature's filters, climates may change, but balance will still occur, one way or another. When trees are destroyed and not replaced, the air does not filter from carbon dioxide to oxygen.

And when that occurs, other things grow instead, creating a balance of sorts. When jungles disappear, nature's water filters also disappear. Water is critical to balance, just like rain cleanses the air of pollution.

Balance is all around us. For balance at this moment in time, it is important that we as humans do our best to maintain balance in nature.

What is given to me is balance is bigger than we think.

Balance is the great equalizer. When dinosaurs roamed the earth and began destroying balance in nature by destruction or eating and killing everything in sight, along came a grand equalizer, changing nature as we know it at that time, and dinosaurs could not exist no longer. Only a few creatures survived. But then evolution, or balance, created a new balance by humans developing and evolving over eons of time.

We cannot be so naïve as to believe that is not happening now. Balance will continue to occur. It is up to the current creatures here to respect nature as much as we can. Ignoring nature and balance only speeds up the process.

The reality of balance? I am told we can kill ourselves off unnaturally or do the same by ignoring balance and nature. Change through balance will occur naturally, but we, as stewards of nature, as creatures of nature, can control balance at least a bit. Humans will evolve into something or someone else in time. And time is balance in itself. For example, humans are getting taller. Why? Not sure, but Americans are taller than a century ago. There are those who would like to say it's diet. In the past, all foods were natural and not fertilized with growth hormones, unnaturally. Maybe we are just being fertilized by what we eat. Balance is ongoing. Our habits are countered with balance.

The spirits are making sure I understand the inevitability of balance. It is not a bad thing. It is a natural and beautiful occurrence. Balance is the perfection of life as we know it. The spirits all know and understand the beauty of nature and the balance needed for nature to "keep its sanity." Nature controls everything here as we know it. Nature is balance, and it is bigger than life itself. For nature controls each day with night. Nature controls each summer with winter. Nature controls each species with another in nature to create an ongoing balance.

Nature will never stop. It is the grand balance of everything, the ultimate law as we here call rules of living. Whatever we try to do or change, nature can stop anything immediately. It is all so powerful. This is nature's house. And each dimension has its own nature, its own natural ruler of sorts. Nature is everything working together in the reality of its own existence. Dinosaurs were here, and then they were not. Aliens were here in abundance, and then they were not. Everything in the past was here, and then it was not. An era was here, and then it was not.

What is the only thing that exists through all of time? The balance of nature. Lest we not forget.

The spirits are glad for the question and glad to have answered. The truth was told directly from the Everywhere.

Balance is everything.

Peace and love to all.

A Basket of Lessons

Interesting morning. I sit down not knowing what will happen, as nothing is coming to me. I wait after saying good morning, as they are all calmly visiting with one another, but no one has come forward to greet me. Even Pap is here but busy visiting.

I ask myself, do I take the day off? The answer is a resounding, "*No …* just ask a question."

So I say beside the body/vessel that I am housed in, "Is there a difference between you and me?" The spirit turns to me calmly and says, "Well, of course." Now I am puzzled and a bit confused. I assumed I was the same and just wanted a verification.

I am speechless and don't know what to say. A spirit comes forward to answer almost like a representative of everyone else. It's as if she is the spokesperson. And I have identified her as a female. She appears to be worldly, educated, mature, and articulate as she stands before me. I can sense a calmness of knowing and knowledge. Her powerful presence is humbling yet kind. It's as if she is a queen that commands respect and honor, yet she almost feels like a grandmother. Her energy is overwhelming. I seem to be speechless.

She speaks by touch. Her smile is absorbing like an aura around her. It's as if she is the designated authority for the answer. Wow … I don't see her eyes, but I can feel her eyes on me. Not sure that makes any sense. I can feel her touch but can't see a body. I can feel her truth and love as it is all around me. After all, she is today's spokesperson of the Everywhere.

Here is what I am getting. Each of us here on our journey has a body. Each body has a nerve center (brain) that carries the knowledge and the ability to reason through most everything to needed to survive and live on this journey. We have the capacity to use our brains to learn as much as we can. We can go to school and learn theory. We also learn by watching others as well as through life's lessons. It is a universal way of learning. And our brain magically remembers. It is an overwhelming miracle of sorts to just think of how a brain really works. Yes, we can prod the brain and say this section is for speech, and this section is for other senses, and this section is for memory, short and long-term.

But how it really works we can only imagine. Yet, the brain for us here on this journey is the center of our being. It has been provided to us to learn and bring back information for all in the Everywhere to experience through the immediate connection when we return. It's as if a basket of learning was gathered, and our lessons are brought back to the Everywhere. Like gathering eggs in the chicken house. Each egg is a lesson we add to our basket.

Where we are different than spirit resides in the Everywhere. If we think of the brain, or nerve center and all its responsibilities, there is one part that is missing. It is the all-knowing part.

To best understand, it's like we as spirits are all plugged in and automatically connect to the Everywhere when we are home in the Everywhere. But when it's time to go on our journey, the part of all-knowing is unplugged while on the journey. We have the ability to learn a lesson or lessons while on our journey. There is no need to learn while in the Everywhere, as every spirit is all-knowing.

But when it's time to go on a journey, the learning is activated and the all-knowing is inactivated. Almost like a trade. By doing this amazing switch, the Everywhere can add new lessons of learning to the Everywhere upon returning. The old saying "you don't know what you are missing" has real meaning. Because when you are on a journey, you really are missing the all-knowing and don't know it.

I laugh at myself as I am absorbing this answer, as she is touching me by her presence. I am learning the concept as best as I can, but I am still not knowing the all-knowing. I am only understanding the all-knowing versus the not knowing. I am almost giggling as she is letting me grasp this. Yet, this makes perfect sense.

I have, in the blink of an eye, been given the explanation to understand and sense the true feeling of knowing that when I return to the Everywhere full of new lessons, I will add to the bucket of learning.

I actually have a sense of confidence now that this has been explained. I also have a sense of appreciation, even more than before, of the beauty and truth of the Everywhere.

Everything is always perfect. There is nothing more perfect than all-knowing, and when each of us return from our journey, we plug in to the all-knowing with our bucket of lessons, and all spirits in the Everywhere are automatically updated to a more perfect all-knowing.

This beautiful spirit now stands before me with a look of satisfaction, as she has provided me an explanation as best as she can, because she is perfect and all-knowing. As I glance out over the horizon of the spirits, I can see the satisfaction from each and every one of them. It's as if they are all looking at me, as if I were a child learning from them. It's as if I am part of them, an extension, so to speak. I guess in a way I am just that, temporarily unplugged. I now know that when I return, I will plug in, and I will no longer just be visiting the Everywhere but will remain in the Everywhere once again until my next journey. It sure is awesome to know that all is perfect.

One of the beautiful gifts of this journey is to have this connection of knowing at least a bit of the answer and realizing that I must make sure I teach everyone the truth about the Everywhere. It is an awesome responsibility, and I will do my best. The Everywhere has asked me to do so on this journey.

To this beautiful spirit before me, thank you for your patience and understanding.

Thank you for your presence.

Thank you for your love and your smiles.

It's a great day in the Everywhere.

Hey, it always is. Peace and love to all.

Close Calls

Good morning to us all.

I step through the door as usual but with just a bit more caution, as I never know if I am going to be along a stream or on a cliff. No matter how easy it is for spirits to maneuver, I am still afraid of heights.

I take a deep breath and then realize I am on an island. It's not very big, about the size of a large farm. This is a bit scary too. I have never been on an island with nothing but water as far as I can see.

A relatively young spirit is suddenly in front of me. I can only sense her youth, as I never can see the body of a spirit, only the presence. She says, "Hello, my name is Bea." She turns and looks around and says, "Isn't this beautiful?"

I say, "Well, yes, it is." The palm trees are breathtaking as their fronds are leaning away from the breeze, and the fauna on the island is perfectly formed. Each plant looks like it was painted here. The beach is pure white sand … wow, such perfection and beauty.

Bea says, "Did you ever want to be on a deserted island?"

I said, "Frankly, not really. But I must say, it is beautiful."

Bea responds, "Here in the Everywhere, we can whenever we want. That's the awesomeness of the Everywhere. We can be where we want to be. Do you wish to stay?" I look at her, puzzled.

Bea says, "Come with me." She literally walks through the portal door, and I follow. She shuts the door for a second and opens the door and reenters, and we are back in the Everywhere. The mountains in the horizon and the beautiful grassy knolls of the Everywhere have lots of spirits sort of waving to me.

Bea says, "There now. Feel more comfortable?" I acknowledge that I do. She says, "Good. After all, you have a lot to do on your journey."

I was a little perplexed by Bea's comment and said, "Why did you ask me that question?"

Bea answers, "Everyone on a journey has many options occur where they can return. That was the point of what just happened. You could have opted to return in an instant and could have been on a deserted island or here on a wish. Returning to the Everywhere is an option always. You, as others, always have things happen suddenly where you could make the return occur."

I said, "It's that easy?"

She said, "Ever have an accident or really hurt yourself? Or have a 'close call,' as they say? Did you ever wonder what or where the term 'close call' came from? What did you think that meant?

"A call to return to the Everywhere, of course." Bea says, "You did not have a close call today, but I just wanted you to better understand the door or portal that you come through each day is nothing more than a veil of sorts. You are here now, and you can be there now. Crossing over is really that easy and beautiful."

I said, "I hear of others saying they had a close call and saw a bright light."

She said, "Well, that can be the sense a human might have, but that only occurs because you may be to the point where you are dropping, or almost dropping, your cloak of a body to return. The brightness of the Everywhere may give you that sense. It's like being in a dark room and then turning on a spotlight. Your eyes must adjust to the light, right?

"That's a great way of experiencing the term *crossing over*. When it's really going from your journey to the Everywhere. Everything gets clearer and brighter when you do. The term 'close call' really means returning."

Bea is full of understanding today. I say, "You seem to be so knowledgeable and yet so young."

Bea smiles and says, "As a human, you are forgetful. Remember, I only appear today from my last journey. I was a college student and died from a brutal attack and returned to the Everywhere. I had a good journey, and yes, it may seem to have been cut off abruptly by what happened, but it was my choice to return. I had the close call, and on this journey, I made the choice to return earlier than some might have. It was part of my lesson to others. All is well, and I am back in the Everywhere till the next journey.

"I just wanted to be on a deserted island for a bit, just to see what it was like to be at peace with everything Everywhere. And frankly, it was perfect for me. And then you entered through the portal. Then the island wasn't deserted. So I simply asked, and the look on your face was answer enough for me. I enjoyed the beauty and the peace, but to be here with all the other spirits is wonderful, beautiful, and frankly, just as peaceful."

"Bea, let me ask, what were you going to teach me today?" She looks at me as if I am the dumbest human on earth.

She says, "I just did. Did you not learn a thing today?" Needless to say, my face is red.

I then respond with, "Well, I guess I deserve that. Everything this morning has happened so naturally. I guess I thought there was to be more."

Bea says, "What you just learned is one of the big questions each human is confronted with while on their journeys.

"What's the process of life and passing away? Now there is another term—passing away. Humans know, but they don't. The term 'passing away' is also just as clear as a close call. It's about leaving your journey and returning to the Everywhere.

"You can have a close call, or you can pass away. Both are choices each has on a journey. Close call is almost passing away. That is all. It's that simple and painless. A human has to decide from time to time.

"Always remember, being a human is only a choice of the journey. Being in the Everywhere is the reality of it all. This is where everything begins and ends. And yet, there is really no end, just returning.

"The Everywhere has always been here and always will be. The only thing that is temporary for humans is the existence of being human, and then from a close call or just passing away, you are back to the Everywhere as if it were the beginning, because that is where each of you started.

"It's just being a human seems to be so confusing. Remember, all our knowledge leaves us temporarily as we become humans to learn lessons.

"Your lesson today has been profound. To you and to others as you perform your responsibility in the wave." Bea smiles and then says, "Make sure you have a great day today."

May peace be with you. Love to all.

Lamar the Philosopher

Good morning to all …

It's a new dawn. It's a new day. Yet there is so much to learn from the past.

Wow. Now that I have learned there are no boundaries to the Everywhere, more questions come to me. On a clear night, when I look to the sky, I see thousands of stars. And yet I now know there are more. More than I can see. It's amazing to grasp the wholeness of the Everywhere. Yet I can't see any planets.

Are there more planets than stars?

Not a second goes by, and a scholarly man slowly and deliberately approaches in a robe and cap. His name is Lamar. He is not in sleepwear but in a PhD type of robe and cap with many colors on his yoke. Lamar is a studied spirit, a guru of sorts. He is one who has pondered the existence of the Everywhere. He is a philosopher, as we say. He studied and taught at many leading universities around the world over many decades. He is different from most spirits. He actually had similar paths in many journeys.

My first reaction is, "Why are you so different? What about balance? What about the agreements? What about fairness to other spirits? Do you have preferential treatment, having a similar journey many times?"

Lamar speaks softly but sternly and with reverence. He says, "Having the same journey, frankly, is not fair. You are correct. Yet there is nothing more for me than to do something different. I would love to have a varied and balanced journey. It would be wonderful. Frankly, it is not fun with the same assignment. But I have yet to complete a journey. It's like I am in a revolving cycle of sameness. Being a philosopher, of sorts, I never can seem to get the answer. I only can come up with the questions.

"My assignment, every journey, is to find the answer. Can you assist me today?

"Your question today was encouraging. Are there more planets than stars? Well I have been trying to answer that question on my journey for journeys, so to speak. It is one of the most difficult, maybe impossible questions to answer. It's like the orbit of the earth. Every year at the same time, it's always in the same place in the universe. Yet it's always traveling. So, is the earth moving as rapidly as we say, or is it just running in place? These are the questions I, as a philosopher, am always burdened with. And for me to have a normal journey, my assignment is to find the answer.

"I would love to be a ditch digger, or a farmer, or trash collector in a neighborhood. I don't care. I would just like to be anything but a philosopher. And to do so, I must find an answer, that's all. You are not the only one I have asked. First, I ask myself every day. I ask here and on my journeys. It's never ending like the traveling earth that doesn't travel?

"Descartes once asked, 'If I take a half step halfway closer to the wall each time, will I ever reach the wall?' Just guess who that was. Hello?

"If you ever get an opportunity to select your path, your journey, and the topic of philosopher comes up, do not say yes. It's not as glamorous as you may think. I know, everyone jokes about being a philosopher of sorts. Must be an easy job to sit around and think about things all day. Well, it was at first. And then maybe the second time. But just give me an answer, and I'll dig ditches. Please, please."

"Okay, Lamar, now I am a bit confused. I thought everyone knew everything in the Everywhere."

Lamar says, "Well, yes, the Everywhere is all-knowing, all-powerful, and all-loving. Yet, let me remind you that every journey is to learn more so the Everywhere continues to be all-knowing."

So then I ask, "Well, if the Everywhere is all-knowing, then why does it still want to learn more?"

Lamar laughs and says, "Welcome to my world. The torture for a philosopher is being a philosopher. There are still questions to be asked and answers to be found. Learning is ongoing. That is why humans must study history. You can't know where you are going unless you know where you came from. That question in itself has an ongoing answer."

"Lamar, so what can come of my question to you today? There seems to be no way you can answer it for me. Can you at least try to give me a hint as to the number of planets versus stars? More or less?"

Lamar says, "Not sure, but I can give you a clue. First, you can't have a planet without a star to orbit. There must be at least one planet per star, if not more. After all, there are eight or nine planets that orbit your sun, with the sun being a star that is like the mother to the planets. They cannot exist without a star to orbit. Not sure, but I suspect that is where meteors come from. Former planets or stars, or moons that tried to run away. Now that is a thought. Are moons like children trying to run away and play? If so, I guess they find the answer too late and become a meteor? Oh my? That is a sad thought."

"We may be getting somewhere here, Lamar. So, if a planet can't exist without a star, does that mean yes, there are more planets than stars? Or are there stars without planets?"

Lamar says, "Maybe the moons are planets in waiting. They are learning to be a planet to run away and join another star? Hmm. Now that is a thought too. As you can see, being a philosopher is like trying to learn what can't be learned. There seems to be no real answer, and yet, shouldn't every question have an answer?

"Here we go again," says Lamar. "I feel like a philosopher that can't philosophize. Now that's a play on words. At least I can keep my sense of humor."

I get Lamar's attention and ask him one more time. "Look at me, Lamar. Focus on me. I have a question. I have learned that there is no boundary to the Everywhere. The universe as we know it is the Everywhere, and it has no boundaries. It is all-inclusive. Question … if there are no boundaries and the Everywhere is all-inclusive, then the number of planets and stars can't be determined because there are no boundaries. Right? Can you answer that for me, Lamar?"

Lamar looks at me with astonishment and says, "Since there are no boundaries to the Everywhere, then asking for a boundary to the answer can't be answered. There is no answer, and *that* is the answer." Lamar screams in joy. He answered the question with an answer. There is no answer. It is never ending, which *is* the answer. He can now be a ditch digger or whatever. He is elated. He hugs me with the most wonderful feeling of accomplishment.

Lamar's circle of philosophizing is over. He can now move on with a journey by not being stuck in the loop. He has now completed his journey of journeys. He is jumping for joy. And then he runs into the huge crowd of spirits with all the love and excitement for his future. After all, his future is undecided. He has no clue what his next journey will be, and that's the beauty of the Everywhere ... still learning more that needs to be learned. Because learning is never ending.

And yet it is the most powerful of all.

Family, love, honor, trust, and peace. The big five are still the basics of life, but there is still more to learn.

Peace and love to all. Lamar is a happy spirit today.

Cloaks

Good morning to us all.

"Pap, oh Pap! Where are you?" He laughed as he appeared almost instantly as I opened the door. I see he is at it again with the spacing issues. "Okay, Pap, you have my attention. What went on yesterday? I had two spirits giving me solid visits—and then poof! All gone. What happened?"

Pap smiled and said, "It seemed like maybe your visit was being a bit embellished yesterday, so we just sent a very quiet message. No one is angry at you, as you may have thought. Anger is not in our vocabulary here. No reason to be angry. And besides, what you are doing has an occupational hazard that goes with the territory, so to speak. It's easy to fall prey to expanding a message."

"But I was just asking a question that was given to me to ask. To me, the answer is given clearly every day. Yes, there is life after death. Just my being here with you is enough, but there are some who just want the question asked directly and a direct answer without lessons attached. That was all I was doing yesterday."

Pap says, "All right already," and laughs again.

Pap goes on. "Let's get this out of the way. So, you wish to find the answer. Is there life after death? Okay, I'll answer it with a simple statement that should be easy to understand. Humans are spirits cloaked and burdened with a human body while on a journey. You want it clear? That's clear! Haven't we said that six ways from Sunday, as humans say?

"Spirits don't want to minimize the importance of the human body, as it is necessary for lessons to learn as humans. As a spirit, everything is all-knowing. Spirits know everything there is to know. But as a philosopher says, 'Is there more?' There is always more to learn. Learning should be a constant, and as spirits, we always strive to know all. We just have to challenge ourselves to make sure we know *all*. Yes, learning for spirits mostly occurs when on journeys. Humans are important to spirits too. They depend on each other, I guess you could say."

"Thanks, Pap! I have to ask another question that goes with this explanation.

Am I to understand then that humans are important, and it is the only way spirits can learn? By being human on a journey?"

Pap says, "Listen to what I said. Spirits can only learn when on journeys and are always learning any which way they can. They learn in this dimension as well as others. As an example, your dimension is much more than just earth. There is a lot to learn and understand as a living being. Just imagine how much there is to learn as a spirit. Yes, spirits are all-knowing, but knowing (learning) is constant and everywhere to the Everywhere."

Pap continues, "You have discussed the largeness of the Everywhere. It's never-ending, which includes all directions and all dimensions. As a human, you can only clearly imagine one dimension. You may try to understand other dimensions, but it is not clear to you. As a spirit in the Everywhere, we are all-knowing, and by the way, that includes every dimension. Remember spirits are here, as in *now*, and there as in *now,* and everywhere as in *now*. Being here and there is instant for spirits. There is no time in travel for spirits because time does not exist. Humans must figure out a way to load up the body to move it. Humans need horses, carriages, bikes, cars, trains or … I could go on and on, but humans must figure out how to carry themselves from point A to point B because of your bodies, your cloaks.

"Consider your human body as a coat. When you take your coat off and hang it up to store, what are you? A human? Of course not. You are a spirit and here in the everywhere. How difficult is that to understand?

"Spirits have journeys in many ways and materialize in any way needed to learn. They can learn as humans, animals, bugs, trees, or any other way necessary. After all, spirits are everywhere. And remember, there is no time in the Everywhere, so a visit as a human can be a lifetime to a human. A visit as a human to a spirit is like here and there. It is that quick as a spirit. Spirits are constantly learning.

"I know this may be most difficult to absorb and grasp as a human. It's meant to be challenging to understand. Religions try to teach it and do their best, but what about atheists? Well, they bring back their lessons too.

"Everything is important, has meaning, and is a lesson. Nothing happens by accident. Every second is a lesson in life as a human.

"And yet it's natural for a human to believe all this and yet, simultaneously, doubt it even to the last second before removing the cloak of the body. It's a human trait to always question and learn and doubt. That is how learning takes place. So, Billy, even the humans who get it as you do, will always have a smidgeon of doubt until the human life is officially ended. In that split second, as you say, when life stops as a human and you are a spirit, then and only then will you return to all-knowing as a spirit.

"The snap of a finger and—voila, spirit again. Surprise! You really didn't die. You continued on as a spirit. Your next journey is ready, and you can go to your next journey or relax as a spirit. Regardless of when or where, spirits are at peace, they are family, they honor the truth, and they love everything everywhere.

"So, don't ask the question about humans on another planet somewhere, or being something else in another dimension. Don't ask because you wouldn't get the answer anyway. After all, you are only human.

"And you should be happy as a human. You have the ability to learn and be a family. Always love, honor, and trust in peace. So, why not go forward and work on that assignment. From what we see here in the Everywhere, you have a lot of work to do. You are part of the wave. Get with the program and do your part. It *is* that important.

"Peace be with you today and always. It's supposed to be the human way too …"

Values and the Wave

Good morning to us all.

Yesterday when I opened the portal, there were five stumps that we all sat on for our discussion. Today, I see no stumps. Yet the stumps were rooted in the ground yesterday. Where are they now? So how did this happen? When I open the portal each day, I assume I will be in the same area in the Everywhere. After all, I am literally in the same ten-square-foot area on my side of the door/portal. Can someone explain to me how this happened?

Appearing in front of me is Uncle Chet. His given human name was Chester Mellot. He was distantly related to me since his mom was my Pap's sister. So, we are cousins of some sort, but I came to know him as "Uncle." I had "uncles" all over. And frankly, each uncle was as loving and friendly and "uncle-ish" as you would expect. Always glad to see me. He was at nearly every family function, dinner, reunion, and gathering. Every anniversary too. It's funny, now that I think of it. Birthdays were not a big deal in our family circles, but anniversaries were. Every twenty-fifth or fiftieth anniversary was celebrated and well attended. And I mean we all attended. There were dozens and dozens who would show up. And Uncle Chet was always there with his loving and gracious wife, Aunt Romaine. What a great couple. They were farmers too, and poor as could be but rich in so many ways. They could not have children, as I remember, but they adopted a son named Rick who was every bit part of our family as anyone else. He is a great cousin to me, as we have continued to share friendship over the years.

But back to the question of the day. "Uncle Chet, I'll bet you can explain."

He smiles and says, "It's so easy to explain it's complicated." And he looks around to the others, and they are smiling as they nod in agreement. It is interesting to note, and I don't comment mostly, but these visits each morning have drawn many spirits to our discussions, as if they traveled to be here. And as far as I can see, they are here and attentive. I can't imagine that my visit is that important to most, but they sure seem to be interested as if it were. It's an amazing feeling with so much love and support coming from everyone.

Uncle Chet says, "Here in the Everywhere, if we want to be here, we are. If we want to be there, we are. There is no time here, so there is no distance because it takes time to explain distance. Yes, humans look at the distance to go from one area to another. And when they visualize the distance, they try to attach the time it takes to get from point A to point B in a way they understand. For example, it's almost three thousand earth miles from the East Coast to the West Coast of the United States. Humans visualize it takes about four to five hours, currently, to travel by plane, or about four to five days to drive by car. Humans seem to attach time to distance.

"Spirits here can be here or there, in, well, that fast! In an instant. In a blink. So Everywhere can literally be Everywhere almost simultaneously. So if I wish to be here with you or, for example, on the planet you refer to, which is 1.3 trillion earth miles from earth, I can be there now if I wish. Just like that!

"So, to answer your question, is the portal the same place every day when you open the door? The answer is always, sort of. It's here, there, and Everywhere all at the same time. See how simple yet complicated it is?

"For you to understand, it may be difficult, as you always connect distance to time, right? But when your journey is over, you will immediately be here with me or there with me and everyone else always at the same time, same place, so to speak. It's great!

"After all, as you know, I did not travel much when on my journey. In fact, the only time I ever left Pennsylvania was when I went to war as a soldier, like many of us did back in the day."

"Uncle Chet, I was born right after World War II, but I do remember those referring to you as a war hero. What did you do?"

Uncle Chet looks at me with love and firmly says, "Billy, I was no more a hero than anyone else. We were all heroes in a way. For every one of us who went to fight in Europe, there were those who were told to stay behind and help in any way they could. They had victory gardens to provide food. Some supported us by working in factories or wrote letters to those who were serving.

"Everyone fought in that war. Every American had a stake in that war. It was freedom that was at stake. The love of family, honor, trust, and peace were at stake. We all had to fight war to have peace, if that makes any sense. So, was I a hero? Not anymore than everyone else. We were all there to stop the war and have freedom and peace for everyone.

"Nothing else needs to be said about World War II. But you are facing similar issues right now as. It may seem different to you, but it is the same. You are fighting for the same reasons we did back then. And it will take every effort from every one of you to fight for the same reasons. Family, love, trust, honor, and peace. And yes, it's worth fighting for. After all, what else is there?

"It's what you brought with you to your journey, and it's all that you will return with. And life on earth as a human provides the lessons to learn the values. Nothing else is important, although power, greed, and sins of your times get in the way. That is your war.

"Fight for what is right and just. The simple values of life itself are at stake for humans.

"Of course, we support you. Of course, we will teach you. Of course, we will do everything we can to assist.

"But you and others must carry the torch for what life is all about.

"The wave is upon you, as *you* are part of the wave.

"Your journey was created as a part of the wave.

"Your life has been directed to do just that, as others around you have also. You and Susie are together now for a reason. You must move forward with the wave and find others to join you in the fight for what is right.

"You must bring back family, love, honor, trust, and peace where it's missing. You must find it and make everyone see clearly how simple yet complicated it is. It is worth everything on earth, as it is everything here in the Everywhere.

"You too can be a hero. And so can everyone else. You have a cause to fight for. It's worth everything. And it's at stake more than ever before.

"So, go forth and fight on your journey. Teach what needs to be taught. Touch everyone you meet. Yes, you have the burden of being human. And as a human, you also have the burden of the truth to carry too.

"Love and peace to you and all. It's been great being with you today … Here, there, and Everywhere. Oh, and yes, Aunt Romaine sends her love to you. She is here today! Hey, that was a joke; if you look around you will see her. She is here now. It's not as complicated as you think. Keep on smiling."

Continued Learning

Good morning to us all.

I opened the door this morning, and I am on top of a mountain. Frankly, it's pretty high, and I can see both sides of the mountain. There are valleys of course in both directions, and they are beautiful. There are groves of trees or small woods scattered throughout each, with a medium-sized creek winding through. This is just beautiful. I can see spirits walking about, sitting by the woods. They are all around, and they are coming down both sides of the mountain.

However, I don't see one spirit climbing the mountain to the top. I stop and study that phenomena, and yes, every spirit on the mountain is either standing, sitting on a stump or a bench, or climbing down the mountain. They don't seem to be appearing from anywhere, just there. I am puzzled now.

"Excuse me, can I ask a question please?" Two spirits walk up.

Marta identifies herself first, and then Allan says hello. Marta says, "Sure be glad to answer your question." Of course, I have learned now there is no need to ask again because Marta knew the question. She says, "You are correct. No spirit is climbing a mountain. There is no need to climb a mountain in the Everywhere. If Allan and I or any other spirit wishes to be on top of the mountain, we are on top of the mountain. We wish to be somewhere, and we are there. Remember, climbing a mountain takes time, and there is no time in the Everywhere."

"So, Allan, when I open my door each morning, especially lately, I never know where I will be. Why am I on top of the mountain today?"

Allan smiles and says, "What did you see the first time you opened the door?" And I responded with a beautiful view with mountains all around in the horizon, with spirits pouring down the sides as if they were walking to me.

Allan smiles and says, "Then you know where you are. You are at the top of the horizon today. Isn't it beautiful? You can still see the mountains in the horizon too, can't you?" I must say, this is a bit amazing, but then, everything here is amazing.

"As a spirit, do you rest or sleep?"

Allan looks to Marta, and they both chuckle.

Marta, says, "No, why would we sleep? There is no need to rest." This is an interesting day for me, as I have been lucky enough to meet with spirits for some time now, and yet I have never asked these simple questions before.

Again, Allan smiles and says, "Uh, you have been meeting with spirits forever. You may not have realized that in the past, but you are always with spirits every day.

"You are not visiting the Everywhere. You are just on a journey now and directly connected from your journey. That's the agreement for you this time. You are part of the wave. This is an important journey for you. Not that other journeys were not important. You, Marta, and I are always learning on our journeys. You may think you are visiting the Everywhere. And you only feel that way because you are cloaked in a human shell at this time. But you are a spirit just as we are. Let me remind you, when you don the cloak of a human, you lose all your knowledge as a spirit … it's kind of a way to keep your sanity and continue to learn. After all, if you didn't lose your knowledge while on a journey, why would you want to learn when you know everything at that time? So not knowing anything when your journey begins is an important part of your journey. It makes you want to learn about everything you can."

More questions then. "Don't you ever get tired by not getting any sleep or rest?"

Marta says, "Why would we get tired? We are not carrying a body around. Without a body to lug around, there is no reason to be tired. We don't need energy. We are energy, so to speak. We are everything we need to be. The only thing missing for a spirit is more learning. We go on journeys to learn. Journeys would not need to exist if we did not need to learn more."

"So, are you saying humans would not exist if there were no journeys?"

Allan laughs, as we are philosophizing now. He says, "Think about what you asked. All the planets and dimensions of each are there to learn more. And yes, if we did not need to learn more, they would not exist. There would be no need. But spirits exist to learn. It's the core of the Everywhere. And spirits are the Everywhere. So planets and dimensions are there and will always be there because we spirits are always learning.

"However, learning requires the journeys to earn and learn, so to speak.

"Do you see any dinosaurs walking around on earth? They lost the ability to survive. A new set of journeys took over, so to speak. Humans came along, and dinosaurs disappeared. It just happens."

"If I understand you, humans are here until they are not, correct?" Allan and Marta both nod in agreement.

Wow, that is an eye-opener for me. Marta says, "It's no different than before. Humans must earn the ability to learn, or there is no need to exist anymore, just like the dinosaurs. It's quite simple.

"Your existence as humans is only dependent on your abilities to keep learning to earn your existence. You have to learn how to keep surviving. That is why you are part of the wave. You are there to make sure humans keep learning, and then if they do, they deserve to still be. It's like self-preservation as a species, so to speak.

"In a way, you are the same as a dinosaur. Make a mistake as human and stop learning, and earth will no longer be your home as a destination for a journey as a human. Earth will still be there but maybe in a different sense or dimension. Earth is a house for journeys who learn to earn.

"Don't take it personally, but earth is like other planets. It's a house for journeys as a spirit. We love the earth, and we love going on a journey as a human. But we also love journeys in other existences too. And you do too. You just can't sense it, as you are cloaked in a human's body right now.

"And when your journey is over, as others' are, you will be here in the Everywhere again with us on the mountain or in the valley or along the streams. Wherever you wish to be you will be. It's beautiful here and such a loving family of families here. And yes, we trust and honor each other in peace. That's all there is here and all there needs to be.

"You left here with this, and you will return with nothing more, except you will bring back more knowledge. After all, that was the purpose of your visit.

"Go back to your wave now and get to work. There is plenty of learning to do. May peace be with you. Just glance over the horizon once more to fully grasp the beauty of the Everywhere. After all, it is awesome.

"Peace and love be with you today."

Vacation

Good morning to us all.

As I open the door today, I notice I am back to the original area that I first entered, which is kind of refreshing. It's as if I am coming home. It's the same feeling that I get when I am returning home from vacation and cross the border into my home state. I always laugh at myself when that feeling occurs, but hey, that's the way I roll, I guess you could say.

However, there are two small changes; at least they seem small to me now. Two stumps are in front of me, and a little trickling stream is nearby. How peaceful!

So I sit down on one stump and take in all the beauty, and then as usual, I see all the spirits relaxed and enjoying the view. It seems as if they are having small gatherings visiting with friends. I see peace and happiness as far as I can see. And yes, in the distance, there are the mountains, and I can see spirits pouring down from the top as usual. It's definitely back home.

As I take a deep breath, suddenly in front of me, sitting on the stump, Marilyn appears. "Hello," she says. "How are you today?"

I say, "I am wonderful, but how did I already know your name?"

She says, "Because I told you just as I was sitting down on the stump."

"But I did not hear you."

She chuckles and says, "You heard me in a different way. Just think about that for a second so you understand."

I am puzzled, and as I am reviewing what just happened, she adds, "Years ago, after your Pap returned to the Everywhere from his journey, did you ever feel his presence?"

"Of course," I say.

"Did you ever feel or sense he spoke to you?"

"Of course."

"Then you heard him, right?"

I nod in agreement.

"So that is how you heard me today."

"Sure is amazing how all this happens. It's like an alternate reality, almost."

She chuckles again. She says laughingly, "No, being a human is the alternate reality. You just can't fully sense that because you are cloaked in your human body. But you will know when you return from your journey.

"Did you ever hear the term *subconscious?*"

Again, I nod yes.

She then says, "Can a doctor locate the subconscious?"

"I don't think so!"

"It's there, and you can hear your subconscious, right?"

"Sort of, I guess."

She says, "Well, you think about that. Let it sink in, and over time, you may be able to understand more clearly. After all, being in a human body is like being surrounded by clouds. You can almost see, but you can't."

"I did come with a question today."

Marilyn says, "I know." She glances around in a way to let me know that everyone else knows too.

I say, "I keep forgetting about that."

Marilyn says, "Well, there are the clouds again." And everyone within earshot of my comment chuckles.

"My question is, how was the sun created? And how does it keep burning so hot and brightly?"

Marilyn says, "Well, your scientists say it is a ball of gas that keeps burning on the surface, and it is predicted it will someday burn out, right?

Again, I agree. "But how did it get there?"

Marilyn said, "Because it did."

I am lost again.

Marilyn says, "The sun has been there as long as it has been needed. It is your solar system's heat and light source and also the center of your part of existence as a human on earth. If the Everywhere determines its journey is no longer needed, then it will not exist anymore. Just like humans and just like earth."

"But scientists say earth has been here for millions of years."

She says, "There you go again with the time thing. There is no time, remember. The earth and sun have been there as long as it has been there; it's really that simple. And it will exist as long as it does."

"Can you see the stars in the sky on earth?"

"Of course I can."

"Okay, and how long have they been there?"

Marilyn says, "Since they have been there. Since there is no time in the Everywhere, the stars are there, or they are not. It's just that simple."

She looks up. "Do you see any stars in the sky or a sun here?" I look up and realize I do not see any stars or a sun, and yet it is bright all around me. And the beauty all around me is astonishing.

Marilyn says, "So why do you think it is so bright and clean and wonderful here?"

I am puzzled as I say, "I can't answer that question."

Marilyn says, "Because it is the Everywhere, and it always has been the Everywhere because it is. There is no time to measure the Everywhere. Because there is no time, there is no beginning or end. It just is."

"But on earth, you have time. You have a beginning and an end. At least humans do."

"Seems a bit confusing to me."

Marilyn says, "I will use an old saying you humans use. You must have your head in the clouds." We both laugh.

She says, "It's really quite simple here in the Everywhere. The Everywhere is all-inclusive. It is everything and always has been and always will be. There is no time in the Everywhere, and because there is no time, everything in the Everywhere just is and will be.

"However, on earth, there is time, so there is a beginning and an end. Each journey for a human is just like you traveling on your vacation. When you cross the state lines and return to your home state, you have the feeling of being home, right?" I nod in agreement. She says, "Well as a human, when your journey is complete and you return to the Everywhere, you will have the same feeling of returning. You just can't sense that until you return. It's that simple. Being a human is like a vacation of sorts, and then you return to the Everywhere. Until your next journey or, as we infer, your next vacation. Does that make it any easier for you to understand?"

I laugh as I say, "It seems like I am getting my head out of the clouds, just a bit at least."

We all smile, and as I look around to the others, they have paused as if saying, "Here in the Everywhere, you can see forever."

"Peace and love be with you today. Enjoy your vacation." And she smiles.

Fredericko's Gang Life

Good morning to us all.

"Hello. My name is Fredericko. Today I am to visit with you." Fredericko, I can tell, is at ease with himself. I sense he is overwhelmed by his presence in the Everywhere and very happy.

I thank him for visiting today and ask if he has a specific lesson for me since he was destined to speak to me. He appears to be emotional, as I sense some uneasiness from my question. He says, "Yes, I do have a lesson for you, as in a way, I am the lesson. I am one of the spirits who learned the importance of the wave.

"Your assignment along with others is more important than ever before.

"You see, my journey started in a city with lots of people and not much to look forward to. My mother had no job. I have no idea who my father was and never had a father figure. My mom did not finish anything, including her education. I basically had a house to live in most of the time, and my mother did whatever she had to do for attention and money. My mom's only instructions were when I could be home and when I couldn't be home. I was a burden to her. And when I was old enough, I made friends with others who had similar likes and dislikes. None of us had any hopes or dreams because we had no idea what a hope or dream was. I was only in school when a truant officer caught me. I was able to avoid foster homes, as I kept running away until they gave up on me. I ended up with my friends who did the same. We all belonged to a gang and controlled the streets as I grew up. If I wanted something, I took it, as all I needed was a gun or a knife and I had what I wanted. No one liked me but my gang. They were what was important to me. I learned that they were the only ones who I could trust or who cared about me.

"Yes, my life growing up was exciting in a way. We were always just ahead of the cops or the other gangs. And I was good, really good at making sure I had my own back, so to speak.

"By the time I was in my late teens, I was shot a few times, stabbed a few times, but the other guys were not as lucky as me. I killed a few others early in life.

"I got my first prison sentence when I was nineteen. Dealing drugs was my job, and I was good at it. But not quite good enough to avoid being caught. Besides stealing and hustling, all I knew was how to deal. I had my own base of users as if it was my own business. It was pretty easy, as all I had to do was to get someone hooked, and then I owned them, so to speak. Some of the tougher ones, I had them join our gang, and they did much of the stealing and gunning as I got older.

"Jail was not easy, but then it was not hard. I had my rep by the time I got my first sentence. Many knew me from the outside.

"Every time I was released, they sent me to a halfway house. I got food and a roof over my head until I was able to secure my place back in the gang. I was not going to be a ditch digger or dishwasher very long. That is no way to look forward to life.

"Besides, I had respect when I was in the gang. My times in the house were like badges of honor. Yes, honor is definitely misinterpreted in many ways on earth.

"If I wanted love, I took it. If I wanted family, the gang was my family. And if a family member did anything to be mistrusted by the gang, well they just went away, I guess you could say. We had our own laws, and we did whatever we wanted to whoever we wanted to do it to. We were badasses and became even worse every time we went to the house. I had many chances to cross over, as I ate a few bullets from time to time. But I was tough, and crossing over would have been a cop-out as a gang member."

I asked, "Do you think life would have been different if you had a dad?"

Fredericko said, "My dad was my Papi, the leader of our gang. I met him when I was nine. He was nice to me."

"Well, I assume he went to jail from time to time too? What did you do when he was locked up, so to speak?"

"Actually, he did not go to jail. He did not rob or steal or even sell drugs. He was the manager of sorts. He had everyone else take the chances, and they paid with time in the house. He made sure we were taken care of in the house, as he convinced the guards to watch over us. I guess you could say he owned the guards too. He had the power. No one messed with the Papi."

"Wow. What did you do when you got older? Wasn't it more difficult to live that kind of life?"

He laughed and said, "Gang members do not grow old. They die in the streets. Everyone I ever knew died in the streets, except Papi. After I was gone, he disappeared from the gang and moved away. He took lots of money and went to his home country and lived quietly off his savings, I guess you could say.

"A new Papi took over and rules today in the streets."

"So why do you think you were to speak to me today?"

Fredericko said, "Let me be very clear about this. My journey was assigned, and I completed my journey, and what I learned was significant. I had no mom to speak of. I had no father, and Papi was not a father. Honor and trust were misunderstood, and there was no peace, ever. So my journey was a lesson of what it's like to live without value. Frankly, humans speak about hell. For me, hell was living in the streets. It's no way for a human to live. Yet, this is all I knew when on my journey. I survived just like the others. I killed just like the others. I raped just like the others. There is no life; it's pure hell.

"You are part of the wave. This is the biggest lesson you can give. You and others have to move forward with the wave every which way you can. There are many of you assigned to move the wave and get everyone on board. It will not be easy, as for many, they have no base to understand what value really is. That makes your assignment really hard, as living in the streets, you have no understanding of life other than to survive by taking from others. That is no life.

"I know my next journey will be different. As a reminder, balance, as you have learned, will give me an opportunity to learn lessons in a different life. I know my next journey will be much different. Balance will make sure of it. I hope to be part of the wave, but as you know, I will not know of my journey till it's time. And I don't know, like others, when that time comes until it does. Hopefully, I can join you soon on earth to help with the wave.

"I really think this wave is the most important of them all. There are so many humans now who do not have any direction or any family to learn lessons or values. They live like I have never seen before on any of my journeys.

"You have been there too. As you know, your former journeys were not all wonderful lessons, and balance was there to make sure your lessons were learned and rewarded, as mine. But you are part of the wave for sure.

"Do not lose your focus. It's easy to do as a human. You must stay the course, as humans say. Keep moving forward. We spirits are making sure we keep the message going forward as we visit with all who have been given these assignments. You all have your part. Keep the faith. Your lesson is important, as they all are. My lesson was just as important. After all, I am more determined than ever before that on my next journey, I will work harder than ever to make sure the values of life are returned. Humans need value to survive. We all know that.

"We just have to teach humans to know that, as many do not. Hopefully, humans are not at the tipping point that they are too far gone to reverse the previous lack of wave. As we are learning, the lack of wave was devastating to the human race. This wave must be powerful in its message.

"So go forth and continue on your journey. We are all supporting your efforts. You must teach your lessons. You have been blessed with your family on this journey.

"Make sure you pass the lessons along.

"Peace and love be with you. It was my honor to meet with you today."

Distractions

Good morning to us all.

I open the door again to the Everywhere, and I am standing right where I first began the connection. It is so overwhelmingly beautiful; it almost takes your breath away. Yes, everyday it is beautiful, but every now and then, everyone just has to stop and smell the roses, as they say.

So I just take a deep breath and enjoy the surroundings of life and love and happiness all around. You can sense it Everywhere. The world sure has a different feel when there is no strife or stress hanging on your shoulders.

I look to my right, and there is a bench. And of course a spirit is sitting there as if waiting for me.

I laugh, as I should expect nothing less than to be part of a grand plan to learn. So I sit down and say hello. The spirit exudes relaxation and restful presence. He says, "Hello, and how is Billy today?"

Why, it's Mr. McPherson, my old neighbor from my days on the first farm!

He says, "Remember the bench I had by the creek? You and I would just sit there and watch the creek go by. Just the sound of water passing by and how peaceful it was. Well, there is no better description of the Everywhere than that old bench, so I thought it would be fitting if we visited today just like we did then."

I smile and say, "It's a bit different now. Your candy bars that you charged us a nickel for in your little store are much smaller now and cost over two dollars. But they still taste just as good. A Snickers is still a Snickers, but the Clark bars are not around anymore. I sure miss the Clark bars." He laughs and agrees.

Mr. McPherson says, "So, what's on your mind today?"

"Well, Mr. McPherson, there are many things I think about every day. I want to really do a good job with my book to make the wave as valuable as I can. But two topics seem to be surfacing often. There is a flurry of announcements recently about new findings of other similar planets light-years away. That is exciting to many, and yet, in reality, it will hamper local religions here on earth.

"You see, religions, as you and I both know, are interpretations of the Everywhere from a human's point of view. But most importantly, local religion teaches that life as humans know it was created here, and earth is the center of the universe. God created the earth in seven days, as one religion teaches, for example. So there may be those who begin to doubt their beliefs by all the new announcements.

"Not that the truth of reality is not important, but one thing that really has been good for humans is religion, as it anchors a family in the same beliefs. That erosion of belief could potentially tear apart families, and I am trying to teach everyone the value of family as the center of the values of life."

Mr. McPherson says, "Your observations are valid and important. But the true discussion of family may seem to be more complicated when, in reality, it is even simpler to explain. Let's try to get in the weeds and review this.

"First of all, in the Everywhere, all spirits are connected, and each spirit knows all, as our knowledge is all-inclusive. Spirits learn simultaneously as each journey completes because all spirits are part of a great family, as we are all connected by family trees, as a way of saying.

"A great example is you and Pap are connected just like some or most of your relatives are connected in your family tree. You, Susie, your sister, your mom and dad are all connected, especially because of your strong connection with Pap and Nana that will never change here, there, and Everywhere. But as you have noticed, Pap and your family tree here in the Everywhere are connected strongly with other family trees, and all family trees are connected as spirits. So, in essence, spirits are one big happy family, as they say. And when spirits don the cloak of humanism and begin their journey, they only go with family, love, honor, trust, and peace. That's all they take and all they need.

"So your goal, your assignment is to teach this lesson and teach all who will listen and understand that on earth, the five values are all that matter. If each would live by these five values, earth would and could be a wonderful journey for everyone.

"After all, today on earth, some journeys are not as enjoyable as others, yet lessons are learned always, whether good or bad. But lessons don't have to be so varied. Balance can make the adjustments naturally, as the goal is to need less balance by teaching all to follow the five values. Balance would love to not have to work so hard, as they say. It would be much easier for everyone if balance had less extreme to deal with. Don't you think so?"

"Of course I do. It makes so much sense. But my difficulty in teaching this is there are those who may think my books are anti-religious and do not teach the values we grew up with. After all, I am learning that God did not create the earth in seven days. Correct?"

Mr. McPherson says, "In a way, you are correct, but also you are not by what you say.

"The universe and all that is here in the Everywhere has been here forever, as the Everywhere is all-inclusive. But if there ever was a beginning, it had to start somewhere, I guess, so who is to say earth was not created in seven days?

"Religion and beliefs have been around forever and should be. After all, that is a way of life for families over the generations and their way to maintain the five values. Families, over time, have been blessed with the five values, as it is natural for all families to live by these values. You just have to remind everyone of the basics and teach them that everything else is nothing more than a distraction.

"Distractions are just as you would think. They get in the way of reality and truth. With common sense, the five values are known by every human. After all, that is how each of you got there. That is all you had. And as you know, that is all you will leave with. So you must teach that simple lesson. All else does not matter. It just is a distraction. So you must actually teach reality. That is a religion in its own. The religion of reality."

"So when I am asked, 'Is there a God?' what do I say?"

"Well, of course there is a God. God is everything to everybody on earth and in the Everywhere. God is all. It's really that simple.

"We are God. You are God. We all our God. God is from one end of the universe to the other, and there is no end. So God is all to everyone here, there, and Everywhere. God is Everywhere.

"Yes, God is the spirit and the power and the glory. How much simpler of an explanation do you need? That phrase explains it all. That pretty much sums it up in a nutshell. As you know, humans write books about it. The Bible, the Koran, the Torah. And on and on. And each book is wrapped around the same—God is the spirit and the power and the glory. All same, the same in their own interpretation.

"God is all-inclusive and all-powerful. All spirits here in the Everywhere are all-inclusive and all-powerful, as we are all part of god. So make sure you teach all that all religions teach the same. It's like Spanish, French, English, and all the languages are different, but they do the same thing; they communicate the same messages in different ways. But they are the same. All is equal, and all is the same.

"Family, love, trust, honor, and peace are all there is. Teach everyone to look past their personal distractions and get with the program, as they say. I challenge anyone to disagree with what you are teaching, as your lesson is too simple not to understand. However, you must realize that even the simplest things are many times the most difficult to teach because the lessons are so simple to learn.

"Many will question the values because it is so easy to learn. So don't take the five values for granted. Value each and every one of them. Each is just as important as the other.

"Hope you had a great visit today. I know you have other things to ponder, but, after all, they are minor compared to what we discussed today. Peace and love be with you."

Tabitha's Short Journey

Hello and good morning again.

Well the bench is here again. I really like Mr. McPherson's bench, but as I can see, maybe it wasn't Mr. McPherson's bench after all. There is a young girl waiting there for me today. "Hello," I say, and she identifies herself as Tabitha. "Tabitha, why are you here today?"

She chuckles and says, "You know why I am here. Susie had a question, and I am here to answer."

I said, "Well, that is true, and you are most timely. So, do you feel bad because your life on earth was so short? Do you feel your journey was less successful? Do you wish you had more time on earth to enjoy and have fun?"

She looks at me in astonishment. She was surprised at the way I asked the questions. She says, "Let me tell you about my journey, and then we can discuss your question.

"First of all, I was born in the inner city with lots of people all around. I was born not knowing who my dad was, and no one decided to ante up the answer while I was there. That's first and foremost. I don't know if I would have liked my daddy, but I sure would have liked to have had the opportunity, but that frankly just was part of the journey.

"My mom really tried to take good care of me. She did have a job, and when she was at work, I stayed with Mammah mostly. She was my favorite. Mammah would sit with me, and we would talk and visit. Sometimes she would read to me, but mostly she would visit me to teach and keep me occupied. After all, as I would learn, the streets were no place to be. It was okay during a sunny day, because there were a lot of people outside, and we could play in the playground in front of our apartment building. But when we did go to the playground, it was tiring; there were a lot of steps."

"Wow … didn't you have an elevator?"

She said, "Yes, sometimes, when the elevators were working, we would. But mostly they were not. It was an old apartment building. There was one elevator that would work, but someone was always there guarding it, so we could not use that one. He was not much older than me usually, but he would not let us ride the elevator. I think that was his job, and I tried to stay away from him.

"On Sundays, Mammah would take me to church sometimes. That was always fun. People there were always so nice. And we could play and read there. I learned that God was a nice person. He was everyone's friend and savior." She laughed and said, "They really tried to understand the Everywhere, and it was okay. At least they try."

"So how long did you live there?"

"Well," Tabitha says, "I started school and was in the third grade. I was having fun at school for the most part, but it sure was noisy there. A lot of the kids were always screaming, as if they were hard of hearing. Some of the teachers would call them heathens and full of devilment. It was funny in a way. I think the teachers meant well, and they sure did try, but I could tell they had bad days and good days. But for the most part, it was fun. The principal, Mr. Jacobs, was my friend and really nice. I wish he could have been my dad. I guess in a way he was, for a bit at least.

"Living the way I did was not too bad. My friends were okay. They seemed to always want to have fun and play games like I did. Having time with Mammah was my favorite. I wish Mom did not have to work so much. She was always tired. She did not have much time for the men though. She would say they were just sniffing around and up to no good. I thought that was funny. Now I know better."

"What happened that your life was so short?"

She says, "Well, I was outside, actually with my mom. She did have some time, and when she did and was not too tired, she would take me to the playground to be outside. There weren't very many trees and not much grass either, but it was still being outside. I was playing with my friends, and Mom was close by talking to another mom.

"At the front of the playground by the sidewalk, there were a bunch of people hanging around and talking, and then suddenly they began to fight, and then I heard gunshots, only two. The third one is all I remember, and then my journey was over. It was that quick. And that was it. My journey was over."

"Are you sad you did not have more time on earth?"

She looks at me in amazement. "No, not at all. My journey was over, and I am back here in the Everywhere. Look around; this is perfect. Everything is so beautiful. Nature is all around. All is perfect here."

I ask, "What do you think was the purpose of your journey, your lesson to others?"

"Well now, that was a different question than I thought. Everyone there was angry and really mad, as I was killed instantly and innocent of any wrongdoing. My journey there was to attract attention so the police would come in and stop all the violence and try to help everyone see the values of life, like you and I know is so important."

I ask, "Do you feel it helped?"

"A little," she says. "I know the police want to help, but there are not enough of them. They seemed to be disgusted and angry with what happened. But there is a lot of violence. There are not enough dads. More dads would have helped. At least that is what Mammah said to my mom many times. But then she said most men did not deserve to be dads, and they were an insult to fatherhood."

"Do you think other spirits here who had a short time on earth wish they had more time?"

She looks at me again and laughs. "Listen, here is our home. Here is where we belong. We are spirits, and our journeys to earth are for just a short time to learn and sometimes to teach others too. I did what I was to do. My mom and Mammah miss me. But I know they will meet with me again when they return.

"Being on earth for a little or a lot of years may seem like a long time to you, but in the reality of the Everywhere, which is forever, ten, twenty, or eighty years is a blink of an eye. So now I am fine and happy to be home. You can only understand the insignificance of your question when you return and instantly know the answer. Make sure you enjoy your day on earth and make sure you have a peaceful, quiet one too.

"Remember, all things turn out to be perfect. You will see. Love and peace to all …"

Peggy the Parrot

Good morning to us all.

Whoa. I realize when I walked through the portal, I was standing on a limb of a very large tree.

I carefully sit down on the limb and gather my confidence, as I am a bit afraid of heights. In fact, I am very afraid of heights. It is a bit unnerving to enter today with this queasy feeling that comes over me.

I take a deep breath and gather myself. I look around, and as usual, there is beauty everywhere, in all directions. Breathtaking for sure.

Suddenly, to my surprise, Peggy lands by my side. Peggy is a parrot, and her colors are exuding her spirit like I have never seen before. Such brilliancy, almost like a ball of rainbow. Peggy says, "Hello," in a chirpy voice. I just had to say that. I thought it was funny. Peggy reads my mind of course and says, "Yeah, I get that all the time. It's okay. I am used to it."

I say, "So what brings you here today, Peggy?"

She looks at me inquisitively and says, "Really? Susie asked this question yesterday. Don't you remember?"

I sheepishly nod. Then I say, "It is a bit overwhelming to know that all of you know everything about everyone before, during, and probably after anything is said or done."

Peggy says, "Well, how many times do we have to remind you? Are you a human being or something?" She laughs with a chirp. Gotcha!

Anyway, Peggy and I sure do know how to have fun, especially having just met.

Peggy says, "Well, there you go again. Just met? Well yes, but really no. I am from your tree in the Everywhere," and again she laughs. "Get it?" Well, we are having fun today.

I say, "I am not sure I understand. Can you explain?"

Peggy chimes in. "As you know, every spirit in the Everywhere is permanently connected, but some even more than others. There are families of spirits that are like the roots of a tree, and their roots are, of course, connected to all other roots, but the specific roots directly connected are like your family tree. You, Susie, Pap, Nana, and other special relatives and friends are directly connected in your family tree."

I say, "Yes, I understand. I do remember early on in this project the explanation. Sometimes my memory does not directly remember, as I am only the messenger. A spirit provided the message. I only delivered it."

Peggy says, "You don't have to remind me. After all, I can repeat anything I hear. After all, I was a parrot. Get it? I parrot everything," and she laughs again.

"Okay," I say, "so where do you fit in my family tree?"

She says, "Over many journeys, I have been part of your human family or close by. I am a parrot now, but before in other journeys, I was a directly part of your family on earth. I was a great-great-great-uncle of sorts. I was the family clown, as you say. Always full of practical jokes, even back in the early days in your tribe. I suspect Pap picked up my habits, and he mimicked me with his practical jokes. He must have a bit of parrot in him too, as he mimicked me." Peggy laughs again. "Get it? Mimicked? Billy, you seem to be a bit slow today." And she laughs again.

"Peggy, you are quite the jokester and a lot of fun."

Peggy says, "Life as you know it should be fun, and I make sure it always is on my journey. I love to laugh and love to have fun. In fact, if you think about it, your entire family loves to laugh, and they do loudly because laughing is so invigorating. Laughing just makes me want to flap my wings," and she chirps again.

"Oh, stop it," she says with a big chirp.

"So," I say, "how or why did you become a parrot on your last journey?"

She says, "You just become what your journey was meant to be. This time, I was a parrot. Like you have been told before, my cloak given to me was to be a parrot. It's a great honor and fun to be a parrot. I bring love and enjoyment to everyone. No one gives a parrot trouble. Everyone loves a parrot. Did you ever meet a human who was not mesmerized by watching a parrot? All humans love parrots. It's a great life to be loved by everyone.

"I brought joy to everyone around me. It was great. My owner—and I'll put that lightly—was with me almost from birth till I returned to the Everywhere. I watched her grow up, become a lady, get married, have kids, and retire a very happy person. She took me everywhere she could. Even in my later years, I would go with her to the nursing home to visit her mother and friends. Everyone loved me in the home. I had so much fun."

"So," I ask, "spirits become animals and birds on journeys too?"

Peggy looks at me and says, "I wish I still had my claws. I would dig into your arm for having asked such a stupid question. Well, yes, of course. You sure have a lot to learn. It is amazing for you to ask me this question. After all, you were a dog before. Don't you remember? You really have a *rough* time remembering, don't you?" She laughs again.

"Really? I was a dog?"

She says, "Of course, you were a golden Labrador. Not the bravest lab, but you did enjoy being a dog."

"I am not sure I understand. What do you mean, not the bravest dog?"

She says, "Well, all labs are good swimmers, as you know, but you were always a bit squeamish around deep water. You preferred swimming in a creek or shallow river. To this day, you still are squeamish in water, even after you learned how to swim. Right?"

"Yes, that's true, but I never thought of myself as a swimmer. I swim like a rock, as I always struggle with staying afloat. It really scares me, just like sitting in this tree."

She chirps with laughter. She says, "I know. That's why I wanted you to join me today in the tree. I thought it would be fun to watch you be a scaredy cat," and she laughs and flaps her wings again.

"Gotcha. Oh, this is so much fun. Why, it's a hoot! Get it? Care to be an owl someday?" And she laughs again. We are enjoying our fun in the tree today. I feel a bit better now that I have been in the tree for a while.

She says, "When your journey is complete and you return to the Everywhere, all your fears of deep water and high places vanish immediately. You are relieved of all the weaknesses and ills and ails of being a human. You take off the cloak of humanism. Being an animal or a bird and just joining in the love of family and friends. After all, life in the Everywhere is like always being a parrot. Everyone loves you.

"You can flap your wings with happiness and chirp all you want. Because happiness is Everywhere.

"So, being a parrot on earth is like being a messenger of good. I know there are other parrots on earth today joining in the wave, trying to do their part. And dogs and cats and other animals are trying to care for humans. They are all involved in the wave. Animals and birds get it. They know how important it is to teach and be examples of love and family. That's all birds and animals want, love and family. They honor you with their trust and live in peace. They are all around humans, trying to remind them of the simplest things in life. Just being loved and to love. It's really quite amazing that humans have so much difficulty trying to understand and focus on the values of life.

"It's a real puzzle to us all at times. After all, parrots, dogs, cats, and all are just trying to mimic happiness and love. It's the easiest thing to do. I just try to add fun to it too. Just like you did when you were a Labrador. You loved being a dog. And except for being a chicken in deep water, you were a great dog. I just love being a parrot. It's so much fun.

"Well you have learned a lot today. Perhaps you can have a good day and parrot what you learned. So, return to the earth and chirp away. You have a lot to squawk about."

She laughs loudly, and away she goes.

Love and peace to you all.

Have a colorful day!

Being Twins

So peaceful today here in the Everywhere. It's like spring just arrived, and yet I know each day is perfect as the day before and the day after. But today just seems to be an extra-great day. Everyone that I see today as I open the portal seems to have a bit of extra zip in their step, as we would say on earth. It's like the spirits have a lighter flow today.

I take in a deep breath of the pureness, and two lovely spirits come closer as they greet me. "Hello," they say. I acknowledge the beauty of today and that they are a breath of fresh air with their presence today.

One is Alma, and the other is Emma. They are sisters of their past journey. "And yes," Alma says, "we were twins."

Emma says, "But I was born first," and they laugh as if teasing each other.

I say, "How long was your journey in earth years?"

Alma says, "We both lasted eighty-four years." And they both laugh again.

I say, "Wow, that's terrific, but I am not sure you can help me today with my question. I am a bit perplexed, as I know all of you know my questions before I ask. So knowing this, why are you here today? You both seem to be so happy and loving."

Alma says, "We are and always have been, that's true, but we were always surrounded by hate on earth.

"Hate is terrible, as we both know. Our lives were not happy and loving, as we were not with happy and helpful parents. In fact, they were not nice, as our journey was a test for us both. We were punished and beaten as children. Yes, we were mischievous as kids but only for a bit, as we had to go to the fields and work as peasants at an early age. But even then, if we were extra tired and just wanted not to go to the fields, we were beaten and always reminded that we had to do as they wished. Our parents, I believe, had us as children only to be workers in the field. It always seemed that way.

"Our parents' way of living was similar to others in the area. They worked hard as we, did but then at night, they would drink till they fell asleep. We had no parents like others did when we were growing up. They only taught us to work. To the fields we would go. And when it was time for school, our parents tried to keep us in the fields, and many times we would move to other farms to avoid school and keep us in the fields. But the locals would find us and make us go to school. School was our saving many times. We loved to go to school, and we found that learning was fun, and if we learned more than others, we would get praise for our work. So when we went to school, we studied like we worked in the fields. We had lots of fun at recess though. It was our chance to have fun and have friends. In a way, we had the best of both worlds, hard work and play with rewards for our learning.

"And every time we moved, we took with us what we could read and study, and when our parents were out drinking, as they did almost every night, we would read and plan our dreams. We knew our day would come if we kept our focus on learning. It was our way out, so to speak."

"So, did you hate your parents?"

Alma says, "No, hate is not a good way to describe our feelings. We maybe did at first, but there was a time when we saw hate. The workers many times hated the farmers they worked for. It was confusing in a way.

"They would work in the fields, and when they got paid, they got angry. They hated the farmers for taking advantage of their hard work. They always said they should be paid more, but they took what the farmers gave them and went to the trailers or the shacks that were there and would complain and drink and hate more and more.

"And when the hate got so bad, they would move on to another farmer. It seemed like they hated the farmer before they even met the next farmer. It was terrible to see. And when they drank too much, as they did almost every day, they would argue and fight with each other. It was not fun growing up, as we had to be in the fields every chance we had till the farmers had the truant officers come and take us to school. Even the farmers wanted us in school, I think. I always wondered why it was that way. It's as if they wanted us in the fields, but they wanted us in the schools too.

"I was told by my mom that the farmers only wanted us in school to keep the police away from fining them for having us in the fields. It was so confusing at times."

"But how did you end up being as happy as you are today? It's difficult to understand."

"Well, the beatings never stopped until one day," says Emma, "the police came because there was a big fight. They saw us there in the background and noticed our bruises. We were taken away and held for a few days as people questioned us. And then we never returned. They put us in foster homes. And some foster homes were better than others, but they always kept us together. So as long as we had each other, we were happy and working hard in the schools. We ended up going to college, as they gave us scholarships. We worked our way through college and became teachers. We loved teaching and telling kids how much fun it was to learn.

"We met our husbands and had three children each, just like you would think twins would do. We always seemed to be copying each other, and we would laugh about it quite a lot.

"Our lives were great, as we saw hate and desperation when we grew up, and even though we were not rich and wealthy later in our lives, we were rich in love and family. Our husbands did not know much of our past, as we kept that from them. They were good men who worked hard and tried to make our lives happy."

Alma says, "My husband was fire fighter, and eventually he passed from a lung disease. My three kids all grew up to be successful in their own way. I was so happy for them."

Emma says, "My husband was a miner, and he really worked hard in the mines. It was kind of weird that we grew up to be professionals as teachers, and yet we married hardworking men. Kind of holding on to our past in a way. Our husbands were wonderful. My children grew up to be successful. Two of the three became teachers, and one went on to be the mayor of our small town.

"Life was good for us. We grew up among hate, and we lived the life of love as a reward for hard work, as we always said. We could not have survived without each other.

"When Alma decided her journey was over and time to return to the Everywhere, I was right on her heals. We loved each other through the good and the bad, and we are here today together, just enjoying the Everywhere. Being twins taught us a lot. We wish everyone could experience being twins. It is a special bond that cannot be torn apart. Family, love, honor, trust, and peace were always with us as sisters. From before we were born till now and forever. It is a beautiful thing, just like today."

And they stroll on the path and disappear into the Everywhere, smiling and laughing and loving.

May peace and love be with you.

Passing and Returning

Hello and welcome to us all.

"Pap, how are you today? Sorry I have not visited for a few days. Bad back kind of got me out of normalcy with little sleep. But all seems better now."

We hug, as he missed me too. I am not sure how we hugged, but I know we did. You can always tell. Pap's hugs were always long and firm. In fact, it has passed down in the family, as my dad and I do the same.

"Tell me, Pap. Susie wants to know if spirits are returning faster than normal. It seems like so many are passing lately."

Pap says, "No, not at all. It may seem like that in small circles, but it is as it is. There is no rhyme or reason. When journeys are done, they are done. The only time any spikes as you would use the term occur, would be during wars or plagues. Then yes, of course, but it would have to have a humanistic reason for it. Journeys are important for spirits to learn, so there will never be a slow down or a spike.

"Learning is and should be constant in the Everywhere. It is important that spirits are all-knowing, and to do so, constant learning must occur, or all-knowing could not exist. It is a cornerstone of all spirits to know all, be all, and be all-loving too.

"Remember also that not all spirits return in human form. Major, Gabby, Auggie, Seven, and Riley were all spirits returning. You may not remember the monkey I had when you were little, but he too was special and one of our family tree here too. He returned as one of yours, as a matter of fact. But we will let that alone and not be more specific. I know how humans think, and there are those who would misinterpret that information. Spirits are spirits first and foremost. Don't let anyone convince you otherwise. Each one of us dons many cloaks, as a human or animal or bird or other, over all of eternity. Remember, there is no time in the Everywhere. No time is needed to be here, there, or Everywhere. We can be where we want to be when we want to be."

"Pap, do you have to use a black hole, as astronomers seem to think is out there in the Everywhere?"

"There are black holes, but they are not used for travel, as they connect dimensions in a way.

"It's like two pieces of cloth being sewn together. A black hole is the seam between two dimensions, and there are hundreds of black holes. You may be able to see a few as a human, but they are common. The Everywhere is Everywhere, more than a human can imagine. Even your imagination is not big enough to grasp the Everywhere because it is never-ending. And it is as beautiful there as it is here too.

"The best way to explain a journey for you is that it's like a vacation of sorts. Soon, you are going to Florida for vacation, and you will be there for a short time in human terms, right?" I agree. "However, you will do little learning on your vacation, but you will rest and visit with family and friends. Our visits as spirits are similar; we journey, however, not to rest and relax. We journey to learn. Learning is what we do and what we need to be all-knowing all the time. Spirits do not need rest, as we do not need energy. We can do what we want and go wherever we wish because we just do. It's that simple.

"There is no bologna or peanut butter or eggs here in the Everywhere. I know that saddens you," he says as he laughs, "but it's so beautiful here in the Everywhere. There is no time to eat, as we are all so happy and doing what we want, except sitting at a table eating. We can sit at a table and visit when we want to, but sorry, Billy, no eggs or peanut butter here.

"And for you, no bad back either. There is no pain or ache or disease here in the Everywhere. Just peace, love, honor, trust, and family. That's all we need, and frankly, that's all you need too.

"I know your mom and dad are struggling a bit now. Their journeys will be over soon, and they will return here in the Everywhere. But they have had full and interesting lives. They have learned a lot. And it will be good to have them back from their journey soon. I know you will miss them, but then, you really will not because they will be here with me again. You will continue to see them here too.

"That is the beauty of the Everywhere and why spirits are always happy. Spirits never lose a friend or a family member. They have family and friends forever. It's wonderful. Your mom and dad are completing agreements they made prior to their journey. You must understand and accept this even though it will be difficult. But it is soon to be. They will know when it is time.

"Their brothers and sisters are here waiting for them to return. See, you use the term *passing on* as a term of leaving life as a human. We use the term returning to the Everywhere because the Everywhere is really the reality of life itself.

"Remember, they have been humans, sort of like being on a vacation to learn, and they will return with much knowledge of their visit.

"I leave you today with that wonderful message. When your parents return, they will not leave you behind but will have the opportunity to be with you even more. They will not be separated by miles anymore but only by the blink of an eye, so to speak.

"We love you all and make sure you have a back painless day. Keep smiling, as you say.

"Love to all …"

The Spark[*]

Good morning to us all.

I open the door today to what seems to be the original view when I first connected to the Everywhere. There is the same serene, antique white and green view as I see the horizon with spirits everywhere. You can see happiness and peace as far as the eye can see. It's like a permanent park, if you can imagine. Babbling brooks, groves of trees, and flowers wherever they wish to be. Ironically, I don't see a weed. Now that's funny. No weeds. I don't blame the spirits at all. Besides, who needs landscapers in the Everywhere, right? As I smile thinking of my comedic thoughts, a worldly-looking spirit approaches. He moves with sureness and understanding, as if he is unique. Yet I know spirits are all-knowing, all-powerful, and all-loving. He just has a way about himself, which is flowing, if that makes any sense. He introduces himself as Oscar.

"Nice to meet you, Oscar," I say.

Oscar says, "It is my pleasure. Pap has told me much of you. He says you are one of the good guys, so that's all I need to know. Pap knows all." And we both smile. I glance over to my left and see Pap in the distance enjoying the company of friends and family. I smile as he sees me.

I say, "Tell me about your past, Oscar. Every spirit has a story of learning and wisdom."

Oscar smiles and says, "When I was on earth, I was a psychiatrist and studied the mind. I spent my childhood perplexed about the brain and how it functioned. It was such a mesmerizing topic for me. I could not get over the magic of the mind and its capabilities since it is such a plain blob of mass to observe. I saw my first brain when I was at a museum. It was floating in a fluid of sorts in a jar for public view. Kind of weird, I guess you could say, but there it was in its glory. It seemed so simple, and yet it is so complex. I could not take my focus off of it as I grew up. I tried to read as much as I could, and it was inevitable that I would go to college and study the brain and its workings. And I say workings with tongue in cheek, so to speak, because the brain is just there, and yet it apparently does so much. It was amazing to study.

"I spent my lifetime studying and contemplating answers. My deductions of reason were only supported by opinions of others, yet no one could put their finger on the true answer of its function. We could come up with reasons for dysfunction, but even dysfunction could not be explained physically except for electrical impulses. The brain is amazing, and yet it is not. All my life was devoted to the study of the brain. I wrote many papers and books on the subject. I was considered one of the leaders in psychiatry and medicine for treatment.

"Could we as doctors create or recreate the brain? Never, not in a million years. The puzzle I could never answer is where did the electric impulses come from? There was no generator of power that caused the impulses. There was no magnetic force field creating this energy. And life itself can be contemplated and even created in a test tube, but the spark of life that actually occurs cannot be explained. Two cells join like other cells can be joined, and nothing happens. And yet in some mysterious way, some cells when joined actually pick up a spark of sorts, and life is created. Hmmmm? Still can't reason why one pair of cells does and another pair of cells does not.

"It's that spark or something like a spark that makes the difference. Whatever it does, it creates the human shell, and a brain is the center of the shell. It manages everything in the body efficiently, as if it were possessed to do so. What part of that original two cells decided to be the brain and not the other two parts? They say it's the DNA that does it all. And that is where the science stops at this point. DNA is the only answer that we can justify as a reason. But I suspected all along that it was more.

"I didn't learn the truth until I returned from my journey, and then in a split second upon arrival, I realized the answer, which I knew all along. I just could not see the answer while cloaked in my humanism. It was a spirit that surrounded him/herself with the cloak of humanism all along. That was the difference. Once the agreement in the Everywhere is complete and the spirit gets the assignment, the spirit then cloaks up, so to speak, and goes about learning more, only to return with knowledge. And while cloaked in humanism, it can think and reason for the sake of learning.

"Here is a great example. When your Pap returned to the Everywhere, you still had connections, in a way, with Pap, right? You always felt he was with you. You had thoughts of him and dreams of him, and even when you missed him, you still felt that you were in touch with Pap and connected. Right?"

"Yes, absolutely."

"Well, the reason you were connected is because you were connected. He could, in a blink, be in your thoughts and dreams. Spirits can be wherever they wish to be and connect with other spirits at any time, on a whim if they wish. Pap made a concerted effort to stay connected to you because your assignment was to be here and be part of the wave. You had responsibilities ahead that you did not know, and your Pap was responsible for the connection to prepare you for this day.

"Dreams are a continuation of the Everywhere while cloaked in humanism. Your thoughts of Pap were genuine and real, as you felt them to be genuine and real. They were not something cooked up by the brain. They are direct connections that can occur at any time.

"Those of us who have seen, ghosts can potentially understand. Some see ghosts and others feel ghosts, but they are not ghosts, just connections with spirits in the Everywhere. You can't avoid the connection. If a spirit wants to connect or visit, they can and will at any time because then can.

"It's not anything to be afraid of. It's as natural as dreaming of the past, when in reality, it is just connecting now with a spirit and reviewing the past as if having a conversation.

"How can a human be so pompous as to think they are the center of the universe when they are here today and gone tomorrow? It makes no common sense to be that way. And yet humans do feel that way because it is like a defense mechanism to keep focus on the now and to learn as much as we can.

"I spent my last journey focused on this study only to find that it was a narrow-minded approach to the reality of the Everywhere. Only my return gave me the truth and reality of it all. The Everywhere is where spirits live and exist. We cloak our spirits with humanism only to learn, as if it were a spirit's dream. In fact, the journey on earth seems to be years and years for most. And yet in the spirit's reality, a journey lasts only as long as a dream to the spirit. Remember, there is no time in the Everywhere, so seventy, eighty years, or more is just like a snap of a finger for spirits.

"It sure is great to be back home in the Everywhere where truth exudes all. Honesty and love exist here, and family is truly family here in peace. There are no arguments or strife or disease here. Only perfection for us all. After all, we are all-knowing, all-powerful, and all-loving. No reason not to be here in the Everywhere.

"As they say on earth, everything always turns out to be perfect. And it does.

"Peace and love be with you today and forever. Have a blessed day."

Bad Dreams

Hello and good morning to us all.

Skuda meets me at the portal door this morning. It catches me off guard since she was right there in front of me when I opened the door. She laughed as if she knew she scared me a bit since she was kind of like in my face. I guess I jerked back a bit when she was right there.

I walk over and sit down on a bench with her, as if we knew the plan today. The bench was waiting, and I guess they did know, as they always do. It's like there is a primer for me, and I am in the elementary grades of school here to learn and have my questions answered.

I then say, "Skuda, for the sake of being formal, I will officially ask the question."

She pauses as if waiting and says, "Okay, go ahead."

"Why do humans have bad dreams? It does not seem appropriate for spirits to provide bad dreams for humans. It just doesn't seem to be in a spirit's nature.

Can you explain?"

Skuda smiles and says, "You are absolutely right. Not a single spirit would do that. However, we might sneak up on you at the door when you come to visit, like today." And she laughs. And I do too …

"Let me explain," she says. "Your mind, or subconscious, is like a hallway to the Everywhere. It is kind of like a direct connection. Imagine there is a door at the end of the hallway. That would be the door to the spirits. When you open the door, you will see a bright light, as if the hallway light is on, except the entire hall is ablaze and surrounded with light.

"This is the door you pass through when you return to the Everywhere. There are times when humans open the door prematurely, only to close the door quickly and not complete the entry. You probably have heard stories of this.

"Your portal door is just before the door at the end of the hallway. It is a door we provide for only a few, as you know. And it is easily marked, as you know. You know exactly how to open the door, as we have taught you. But many hallways do not have that door, or it is locked for the time being.

"However, at the other end of the hallway are many doors on both sides. These are doors humans must get used to in the hall in a way but generally visit when they seem to be daydreaming or dreaming when asleep. You can see these doors have no locks and are easy to open. The doors are different in color. There are lighter colors for fun visits, as you can see with the pale and bright doors. And then there are darker colors for those designated for fear and not-so-fun experiences. It's almost like a virtual movie theater of sorts. They seem to be so real sometimes, as you may be able to remember every little detail. This happens when you enter the door and close it behind you. The visit is much more intense. If the door is open and ajar or just halfway open, and you enter and visit, it is just a whim or a thought or a brief daydream, even if it is at night. But when a person goes to bed and relaxes, they have the opportunity, if they get to a stronger level of rest, to enter the hall and visit, so to speak. Most dreams are great, as they can easily open the brightly colored and pretty colored doors. But there are sometimes, when a person has a bad day or watches a scary movie prior to sleep, they carry a different feeling into the hallway. Or maybe they just are afraid of something.

"Fear gives a person the ability to open the more difficult doors that require more emotion to open. The darker doors are heavier and require more effort to open, and the fear seems to be the extra something a person needs to visit these doors. And they open the door with fear, and they enter the room with fear, and fear stays with them during the visit. Use some common sense here. If you do anything in life and you are surrounded by fear, you can almost bet something not so good is going to happen. Well, it is no different when you are in the hallway.

"The same goes for being in a good mood or having a good day. Fear is not present so your day, and your visit to the hallway is full of brightness and happiness. After all, the lack of fear is happiness in every way.

"Think about this for a second. If you have no fear, how can you not be happy?

"You can say that is a Skuda-ism if you wish." And she laughs. "As a matter of fact, if you tell your friends you are having a Skuda kind of day, they will know you are having a good day. Right? Hey, Skuda is a happy word, and that is why my name is Skuda. When on my last journey, I had no dark doors to visit. So, Skuda is a good journey. And that's my story, and I am sticking with it!"

"Thanks, Skuda. Tell me about your last journey."

Skuda says, "I had a wonderful journey. I grew up on a farm and had all the great experiences you would expect. Lots of pets and nothing but fun. I went to school and made friends immediately. Everyone was my friend. Recesses were especially fun, as you would guess.

"And then when I went to middle school and high school, nothing changed; my friends were always there for me, and we always had fun, laughing and talking all the time.

"There was no reason for me to want to change. Life was just fun. I went to college locally and learned to be a teacher for first and second grades. In a way, it was like never having to grow up. I just spent my adult life playing with kids and teaching lessons like being on the farm. They learned a lot about nature and animals and being nice to each other. We never talked about dark-door stuff.

"My kids in school had Skuda days every day. And they loved me and were my friends forever. It was a good day, a good week, and a good year all the time. I only wish others had no dark doors, but I hope I taught them all that if they did have dark doors, to do everything they could to avoid them.

"Good days don't happen by accident. You must work hard, as you would expect to make sure your days are light and lively and full of color, as Skuda would say in class.

"Unfortunately, there are those who live in fear all the time, and their doors are mostly dark, and that is sad. However, if someone can just teach them to look for the bright-colored doors and days, they too can have a Skuda-type day.

"Fear not, for fun is on the other side of the door. Keep smiling and have a Skuda kind of day.

"Peace and love be with you. Here is hoping your hallway is full of colored doors.

"Love to you all."

Renauld the Painter

Good morning to us all.

I open the door to the Everywhere, and there seems to be a different area today. It's as if everything is the same but different. All the spirits are happily roaming around, and suddenly one appears in front of me as if coming from nowhere. His name is Renauld. He is a painter of sorts, as he describes his title.

I am intrigued by his title, "painter." "Did you attend a university to be a painter or did you have natural talent during your entire journey?" I ask.

He says, "Both, of course. Painters do not learn to be a painter like a carpenter learns to work with wood. Painters learn the finer points of painting in the university from masters as they bring their talent given to them.

"Painting is a special gift, just like the gift you have. It was given to me for my journey. And now I am Renauld, famous painter."

"Renauld sounds French. Are you from France?"

"No, not really. Renauld is my painter name, if you will. People recognize my work as Renauld. I decided to have a stage name to protect my privacy and to convince people of my background by using Renauld as a name they would associate with a painter.

"Actually, my name when I arrived on my journey was Carl. So who would have ever followed Carl's path as a painter? So I keep my privacy as Carl Johnson and use my painter name, Renauld, as needed. People recognize me by Renauld when I am in major cities in an art show. But where I come from, no one knows me other than Carl. It's great to have some privacy. And yet I must also hide some of my wealth as a painter too. Most think I am a farmer, as I live on a large farm far from the big cities.

When you live in Montana, being a just plain Carl is normal. So I am just a farmer from Montana.

"Why am I telling you this anyway? How did you get me to spill the beans, as they say?"

"Dunno," I said, "but it is interesting. You have the best of both worlds, I guess you could say. You have a famous side and a private side. How cool is that!"

"Yes, it is, and I would like to keep it that way."

"Did you have the values of life on your journey?"

"Oh yes, in my private life. It's wonderful. I have a great wife and two small children. We live, breathe, and love the values all day long. But when I travel, no one cares, or no one wants to know. They just look to me for my painting. I guess my celebrity is not unlike the greedy and powerful as politicians and actors and actresses. They seem to attract the mantra of the rich and famous."

"Why is that?"

He says, "Well, it's my humble opinion, but I think behind the shell of their celebrity, they know they are just normal like others. They wish to be special and to be like the pretending that goes on in their public lives, where they are always being followed and quoted. Even though their experience has no bearing on what is real. They are just pretending to be famous like the parts they play. It's so sad to be valued as a falsehood.

"I guess you could say I do the same, but in reality, no one asks me of anything other than to enjoy my painting. I have never been asked a question to express my opinion of power or politics. Isn't that interesting? But I suspect if I did, reporters would flock to my character, Renauld, as if I were one of the rich and famous. But I am one of the rich and infamous. After all, I am just Carl in everyday life and love it. I am sure I will have my challenges when my kids get older and go on to school, but I must prepare them. At least I hope I can.

"My values and my family are that important to me. I want my privacy to love and learn with others like you.

"After all, see the actresses who strut in front of cameras with hardly any clothes on? They attract cameras and attention by wearing a cloak of humanism. Yes, it is their assignment on this earth, but in reality, they are almost the anti-wave, as their celebrity is wrapped with falseness and untruths. If everyone knew more about the values and that their cloaks were, well, just cloaks, I wonder what their lives would be like. It's ironic, as when they return, they as spirits are as loving and as wonderful as others. But their story and lessons brought back are of greed and the misuse of power and celebrity.

"I guess it would be a bit embarrassing to a degree. But hey, that is why their visit was another lesson. Just a lesson of how celebrity is so misinterpreted.

"They may have really good-looking cloaks, but when they return to the Everywhere, it's like their cloaks are hung up at the door and they bring little back to learn except what not to be like, I guess.

"So their celebrity is most fleeting, and I am sure no one here cares of their celebrity on earth. At least I know I don't.

"Enjoy your day. I hope you have your privacy today and in the future. Make sure your message is carried on to all.

"Keep smiling."

Moving Forward

Hello and good morning to us all …

Oxi is waiting for me today. I ask, "Are you of Asian descent or from an earlier time? Your name usually identifies areas of the world you come from."

Oxi smiles and says, "I come from the Everywhere. My name was given to me from a human many years ago, before it was determined to be parts of the world."

"Have you not been on a journey since?" I ask.

Oxi responds, "Oh, many times over. But I chose to come to you today as Oxi from an unknown part of the world. My area of journey should have no bearing on the observations I have made."

"Apparently, you bring an important message or statement for me to learn?"

Oxi says, "Why, yes, but ironically, you already knew that, as things sort of reversed this morning from the norm." We both smile, and with a small laugh, we move on.

Oxi says, "Power and greed are intertwined in the fabric of society now. It is the most important part of your message for the wave. The truth becomes paramount in the lessons you teach. Yes, family, love, and honor are just as important, but they usually can come together once the truth is determined. Without truth, nothing can move forward."

I interject with, "But isn't that true with all five values? Other values can exist without the other four."

Oxi replies, "We could talk in circles about this all day long. You are right. But I have been designated to focus on the truth and trust more than the other values today.

"It seems like time on earth is moving fast now, if there is such a thing. It is most unusual for time to be so important, since it is not a factor here in the Everywhere.

"But over time, it appears ideologies have created somewhat of a following in most countries. There are two sides basically in each tribe or country. At least two predominant sides. Humans kind of take a stand and gather behind leaders on both sides, and this is where the power and greed come in.

"You know the old adage of lining up ten persons to tell a story in a line. You begin by whispering a story to the first human, and by the time the story is told ten times and the last person tells the story, it is many times very different from the original story. Sad but true. This happens with humans all the time. Truth and trust are many times innocently avoided by this phenomenon. Even if those ten persons really want to tell the truth, many times the process I just reviewed jades the facts, and the story still ends up different than meant to be. The truth and trust can be clouded even innocently. Humans are weird like that." He laughs. "Spirits study this all the time, and it is still a head shaker to us all.

"When it gets even more difficult is when a person directly hears a statement of truth and then interprets the truth according to their own way of review. It's not necessarily true or false but presented in a twisted way.

"This is happening more and more every day as ideologies spar to have a following for their power needs and greed. Both sides are guilty of this, and it goes on and on.

"And so it goes. These tribes continue to bark at each other with mistruths, and each side gets further apart.

"Power and greed are so overwhelming now. When the truth is verified by 'an independent study,' one side accuses the independent study of slanting the review, and it continues on and on.

"Humans are referring to this today as fake news when it is simply one side barking at the other with additional interpretations and more fake news. So the truth is never really found to learn by.

"This is where you must focus on being prepared when you push forward with your part of the wave.

"Your view is your interpretation of your ideology or religion. We all know religion is a man-made opinion of how life is to be lived and how it got started. None of the religions are supported by fact per se, and yet the Everywhere is supported by the simplest of truth.

"After all, there is no beginning and no end in the Everywhere. It is just everywhere. There is no time or distance in the Everywhere. Humans exist for a short period of time on earth, and yet, since there is no time in the Everywhere, those who question cannot explain the cloaking of humanism as not to be true. After all, each of them will live and die with the cloak, as you can say.

"Spirits are not born. They exist through time, as time does not exist. You can't deny the truth in the Everywhere because the truth and the trust in truth is the only thing that exists in the Everywhere. There are no sides, just the facts of the five values of life.

"And you can't deny the five values are all you bring to earth because we know that is all you can leave with. Stand your ground. And do not let the false statements cloud the truth.

"The sides will try to overcome you for power and greed. They will try to discredit you for their own needs. Yet you are armed with the truth, and trust will prevail. No one can deny the truth. Stand tall but be prepared to continue to stand tall. You have nothing to worry about. The truth is on your side. Trust your roots in the Everywhere. The spirits have provided you with the tools and wisdom to move forward with the wave."

Oxi smiles and says, "You have a great day. Remember, the truth is not cloaked by humanism. The truth will set you free. Heard that before? Of course you have. Because, you guessed it, it's the truth.

"Be wise, safe, loving, and confident of your assignment. This is the cornerstone of the wave.

"Carry your responsibility with honor and peace.

"The Everywhere is all around you, as we say.

"Love and peace to you all."

Global Warming and Mother Nature

I open the door with a question. I do not have to announce my arrival or my question as I have learned, because it's already in the plan for the day.

A spirit has been given the task of putting up with me and all my questions. I recognize the surroundings as the original view, along with the stream added weeks ago. I have to say it sure is beautiful. However, the spirit has not come forward yet. I scan over the horizon and see dozens of spirits enjoying the beauty of the day. It's like a spring day but a bit warmer than spring. No cool breeze but a breeze just the same.

Suddenly I feel a presence behind me and turn to see a beautiful spirit. Majestic in a way, exuding grace and dignity. And of course bringing a wealth of knowledge. Every spirit is all-knowing, all-powerful, all-loving, and all-connected, as we know.

I say hello in the most respectful way I can. This spirit is indeed mystical, magical, and special in every way. She says, "I am Helen. Good morning to you." When she speaks, it's as if harps are playing.

I am in awe of her grace and presence!

Helen says, "And how is William today?"

I say, "I am fine, but could you do me a favor and just call me Bill? I am Just Plain Bill, as my father has taught me."

She smiles and says, "Well, you are anything but just plain, Bill, but okay, Just Plain Bill. That will be fine. Tell me about this question of yours."

"Helen, I am on the fence about all the talk of global warming. Are humans destroying the environment? Will humans destroy the earth unless we do something to correct global warming?"

Helen says, "Yes, I know there are those who firmly believe that if the earth warms a degree or two on average over the next hundred or so years, the earth will change and not be as strong an environment for humans. Therefore, in the eyes of many, global warming is a threat."

Helen smiles, almost with a chuckle, and says, "If humans think they are in charge of their destiny, well, we both know the answer to that comment. After all, humanism is a cloak for our journeys, as you know. We can continue to cloak as humans, dogs, cats, or whatever we wish to be. But humans really don't have a say in the process. Pleeeaaasse! We will make those decisions here in the Everywhere, thank you. Humans can work and work and work to keep the temperature under control every which way you wish. But if Mother Nature decides to have an ice age, for example, guess what? You will have an ice age like you have never witnessed before. It's really that simple. Not a process that humans can control.

"However, you can, as humans, try to make it as comfortable for you as you wish. You can clean up your litter and keep the environment as clean as you can, but do it for the right reasons when you do so."

"Helen, you lost me there. I do not understand."

Helen replies, "You see, there are innocent and honest ways of doing the right thing, and we all agree, that is wonderful. Remember, *family, love, honor, trust, and peace.* Remember that as we review.

"Those who preach and teach global warming are really and truly trying to gather support for themselves, as power and greed seem to be behind all efforts. The powerful and greedy are using global warming to keep their control over the general populations as they leave power. They set up the topic while in power to keep power when their time to lead is over. They have a torch to bear, so to speak.

"I wish it was from the goodness of their hearts, but we all know it's not. Just follow the money.

"Money, money, money. It's only used on earth. Such a test of the will of humanism. Dangle money and power in front of them and watch. It's like putting a worm on a hook in front of a fish. The greedy will bite every time. It's so predictable.

"Always put a question on the trust test first. It's like a filter of sorts. If a question passes the trust test and smells right, it might be a good thing. But for the most part, if something is outside of family, honor, trust, love, and peace, chances are you can't trust it, because most of the time it was developed by humans for a reason. And when there is a reason attached, it usually can't be trusted. There are no attachments to the five values. They stand alone with nothing needed to support. After all, that's all you came to earth with, and that's all you will leave with. That's it. It really is quite simple.

"And never, never think that Mother Nature is not in charge. Or Punxsutawney Phil?" And she laughs. "Just when everyone thought global warming was the reason for such a mild winter in America, guess what? The blizzard of 2017 arrived just days before the first official day of spring. Don't kid yourself. Mother Nature was just sending a message. She is in charge, and if you question this again, she will always respond in a way you will remember.

"Be respectful of Mother Nature. She keeps her houses in order, so to speak."

"Is Mother Nature in charge of all the environments on all the planets?" I ask.

Helen answers, "Mother Nature is in charge of whatever and wherever she wishes to be. It's that simple. No one questions Mother Nature. After all, she is everywhere. And we are here in the Everywhere. So Mother Nature knows every conversation and everything that occurs."

"One last question?"

Helen says, "Sure, why not."

"Okay, have you ever seen Mother Nature?"

Helen looks to the sky and all around calmly and quietly and says, "Sure, look around at all the beauty. Mother Nature is all around you. Everyone sees Mother Nature always."

And Helen says, "So there you have it. And that's the way it is Here, There, and Everywhere."

She gives me sort of a wink and smile and flows away as she says, "Make sure you have a great day. There is no reason not to.

"Peace and love be with you today."

Chernobyl

Good morning to us all.

As I opened the door today, there was a woman waiting for me. She introduced herself as Stradi.

I was a bit surprised, as it was obvious she seemed a bit alarmed and appeared to want to speak with me, as if it were important.

Stradi seems to be in her midthirties. I say hello and ask if there is a problem.

She said Helen mentioned to her yesterday that I had inquired about global warming. And Helen had shared our conversation with her.

I said, "Yes, that is true. Is global warming why you are here?"

She says, "No, no, no, not at all. I am here for other reasons." She has a hard accent, as if from Eastern Europe. Almost too difficult to understand.

Stradi says, "I am from Russia, and I did not survive Chernobyl. My family lived close by, as my husband worked at the plant. We were very successful and prominent Russians back then. I had two kids and my husband, Bori. Life was good, or so we thought. Then, one day, a leak at the atomic plant occurred, and the rods overheated, and within hours, we were all exposed to radiation. We packed and drove out of there as soon as we could, but in days, we were all dead. Our entire family was killed by the accident. I do not know if the government released the truth or not about the accident, but yes, it was an accident, and many hundreds, if not more, died from the exposure. It's like being killed by an invisible ray gun or something. All of a sudden, your skin develops a rash, and then hours later, boom, no more."

"And what does this have to do with global warming?"

Stradi looks at me with surprise. She says global warming is not a worry, as Helen has explained. "But you have many more items to be afraid of. First and foremost would be yourselves. You can easily destroy yourselves as humans with your stupidity and politics.

"You and I both know that power and greed are behind this all. And believe me, it will be power and greed that destroys the human race.

"Did anyone learn anything by Chernobyl and Hiroshima, from the bomb blast?

"Nuclear anything is a killer. And why do so many countries permit any time of nuclear study or medicine or weapons to be developed? Any simple accident can kill hundreds if not more.

"You have no worries to be concerned about Mother Nature. After all, she will do what she wants to do, and none of you will convince her otherwise. But human stupidity? Now that's another story.

"You need to get this information out to the public, as I am not sure what the public really knows.

"All these 'accidents' seem to be slid under the rug, and the details are hidden from the public so the powerful and greedy can reign over the others. It's so sad to see humans act like this.

"They will do anything to keep control. And on top of that, there are crazy leaders looking for attention who will do anything for notoriety. Take your North Korean leader. He is a wacky, deranged person and controls millions of people because he was born to the head of the country. What kind of common sense is that? I know Russia used to do the same, and over a hundred years ago, that story stopped in Russia. Yes, we replace that kind of ruler with the powerful and greedy, and today, we suffer because of it.

"But these secrets kept from the public are so sad. You must draw attention to the truth.

"Yes, we are all happy to be back in the Everywhere where stupidity does not exist. That's for sure. But my journey was created for the purpose of teaching everyone about the dangers that exist, and I think my journey was wasted because the truth was hidden.

"So please, tell my story. Not for my sake but for the sake of all others. I am now happy where I am, as the Everywhere feels like a reward for my terrible journey.

"And yet, we both know, journeys are created for learning, and although we spirits learned, humans apparently did not.

"And on top of that, there are many governments that hide the truth. Your own country does it all the time. Americans are not angels by any sort. They also are run by the greedy and powerful.

"Keep the faith; move forward as fast as you can. Do so honestly and with an open heart. Peace, love, and family be with you. Bring honor to yourself and your family by being honest with your soul.

"Love and peace to you all."

Gossip with Abby

Good morning to us all.

I open the door, and there is a lady sitting on the bench by the brook this morning. All perky and happy to be there, I can tell. I go over by the bench and say, "Hello, are you here to answer my question today?"

She pats the bench seat next to her and says, "Of course I am. Have a seat."

I sit down and smile, and she says, "My name is Abby. I can answer your question as well as anyone." I look at her in astonishment.

"Are you, uh, are you the real Abby?"

She smiles and says, "Would you want someone other than Abby to answer your question? Your Pap knows everyone, and he thought it would be fun if I answered your question." We both laughed, and then she said, "So ask me the question officially so we can get on with it."

I ask, "Do spirits gossip? I mean, all of you know and have learned all the lessons simultaneously, so what do you talk about? I see spirits visiting all the time, and it came to me a few days ago to ask."

Abby says, "Well, first, I am glad you asked. To be perfectly candid with you, we do not gossip, but we do talk about a lot of things. In fact, I am not sure what, if anything, we do not talk about. Sometimes, we talk about what has not happened yet and what we think may or may not happen too. You never know what life brings you, so to speak. We all learn about that each day as humans and as spirits. So, yes, agreements are made, and journeys are planned, but there are always twists and turns on each journey, and each day must create adjustments that even the planning does not predict. The general agreements are always followed, as that is not an option, but the details of what's in the weeds, well, you never know what happens, as they say. Every minor detail of a journey is not necessarily planned, but the lessons to be learned are. The answers to the questions or lessons must be learned as the assigned journey is being completed.

"After all, that is the purpose of the journey. If we did not learn from the journey, then the journey would not be worthwhile, and learning would not be accomplished. So the journey would never have been created."

"Is that what you talk about here in the Everywhere when I see everyone gathered? There is so much happiness here. And love. It's amazing to view from a human's eye." She looks at me with a look of "What did you just say?" She quickly reminds me that I am a spirit like all others, just cloaked in humanism. So I see the same as she does. I blush and agree but try to explain that I understand what I see through the eyes of a human and am not sure I see the same as a spirit.

She chuckles and says, "Well, if that is what you think, so be it, but I assure you the same will be seen without a cloak. After all, it is what it is, as they say."

I ask, "Do you gossip?"

"Well," Abby says, "is this a real Dear Abby question?"

I nod, and she answers with, "Well, no, we do not gossip, as gossip is usually not truthful but falsehoods that are passed around. There are humans who develop their own celebrity by passing gossip along as if it were true. They are looking for much bigger results than what you refer to as gossip. Humans tend to talk about things as if they know secrets they shouldn't or have heard from a source. But as is always the case, the gossip is not verified, so it is not truthful, and that, as you know, is not helpful. It is a waste of everyone's time to gossip because the truth will set you free, remember? No, spirits do not gossip."

"But what puzzles me is that if all spirits know everything, what is there to talk about?"

Abby looks to me in total astonishment and, frankly, seems to be a bit miffed. She says, "Spirits know all, are all-powerful, yes, and we are all-loving. Let's make that perfectly clear.

"And by being all knowing, isn't it wonderful to be able to talk about anything we want that is truthful with no gossip? It's quite refreshing, even for Dear Abby." She laughs and says, "No, I am not miffed. I know everything like all others. You can't get anything past Dear Abby. After years and years as the human Dear Abby, I thought you would know that by now."

She says in the most loving way, "Just imagine, when you know everything like everyone else, just think of all the wonderful things you can talk about. Every conversation is open and honest. Every spirit can express their thoughts to anyone they wish, and although we can't learn anything more in spirit, we can discuss anything we want openly.

"It is important that when spirits cloak as to whatever they cloak into, they are only cloaking to learn more. That is the purpose of cloaking and going on journeys.

"It's also a verification to make sure that if there is anything to learn, and there always is something to learn, every spirit is all-knowing.

"So, there is a method to our madness. Everything has purpose. Each journey has assignments, and every cloaking has a reason.

"Spirits are also busy on journeys to continually learn. And if our conversations ever have a question that comes up, you can bet there is a journey assigned to find the answer. Spirits have plenty to talk (not gossip) about. When you know the truth, gossip is not a topic of discussion. Why would gossip exist in the Everywhere with spirits? It simply is not a possibility. However, humans are all over the topic of gossip. It's like it is in their blood, so to speak.

"Enjoy the time on your journey. You have to be a policeman of sorts and wade through all the gossip and try to teach the truth without gossip. That is your journey as you assist in the wave. You have lots to do and plenty of gossip to avoid.

"Go forth and enjoy yourself. Meanwhile, Dear Abby will be here whenever you need to talk about the truth.

"Have a great day. Peace and love be with you."

Journeys

Good morning to us all.

I open the door and walk out into the area I normally enter. As I look around today, I still am overwhelmed by the natural beauty of the Everywhere. I see spirits enjoying their activity all around me. It's as if they can't see me today, like I am peeking out of a window. I notice today, for the first time, there are no clouds, only blue sky. Is it because there are no clouds? Or just a perfect day? Hmmm … I see Pap in the distance, and he is heading in my direction.

"So good to see you today, Pap," I say. He glides up to me and touches my soul, so to speak, as he has always done.

Pap says, "Enjoying this beautiful day, are you?"

I respond with, "I had a moment to stop and just visit for a bit and observe the perfection in action. Wow!

"So tell me, Pap. Every day, I come to visit, and it's always bright and beautiful. Are there clouds from time to time?"

Pap smiles and says, "No need for clouds here. We have all we need to grow anything we wish. That is if we wanted to."

I ask, "What do spirits eat for food?"

Pap smiles and says, "No need to. We do not have to feed our bodies like humans do. Never any famine or starvation in the Everywhere. All those issues are the results of humanism. The need to survive does not exist here. I thought you would have gathered that already. It's an automatic understanding here in the Everywhere. There is no need or want of anything. All is perfect, you know."

"I never see the sun when I visit, and yet it's always sunny and beautiful here. Do you have sun rises and sunsets?"

Pap says, "No need to. We have no need for light or darkness. It is all perfect here. No need for rest or sleep either. After all, why would you want to sleep through all this beauty? Look around …

"All is well in the Everywhere, always. Just family, love, honor, trust, and peace."

"Do you ever have family reunions here like on earth?"

Pap says, "Well, you know we have family trees here, as you have learned, but all family trees are intertwined and connected with all other family trees. So there is no need for a reunion, as we are always connected and can visit with anyone we wish at any time. And we are constantly visiting and talking and learning as journeys return and journeys begin."

"Have you gone on any new journeys since you returned from earth?"

Pap says, "We all have here, many times over. I know there are some who choose not to do so, and they have that option. But journeys are not taxing or difficult; they just happen, and then they are over, and more learning results from the journeys.

"Learning is a wonderful thing. The more you know, the more you want to learn. It's amazing to know how much there is to learn."

"When you are not on a journey, do you travel here in the Everywhere? I mean, like, are there vacations?"

Pap laughs. "No vacations, as there is no need, but if I wish to travel, and I do all the time, I just travel, and then I am there. Just like the others."

"Whoa. Hold on, Pap. Okay, as I am learning, we humans will need to come up with a plan to travel to other inhabitable planets to raise food and set up other planets for survival. So we have to determine how to travel in a timely manner to do so. Do you know how to do that?"

"Of course I do," says Pap. "All spirits can do so in a heartbeat. But for spirits, it's different. We don't have to drag around cloaks from place to place. We can just be where we want to be when we want to be there. There is no distance in the Everywhere, as you understand distance. You are burdened with the task of learning how to travel. It's part of the learning process for humans and others.

"When you learn how to do so, then we learn from your journeys. We have mastered that from the beginning, and it's important that humans must learn the same to create other learning environments in the future."

"And what if we do not create new learning environments? And we cannot sustain ourselves as humans?"

Pap says, "Then humans will have not been able to survive. It's that simple."

"So, if I understand you, Pap, we could self-destruct our species, so to speak?"

Pap says, "Well, that is true. But you could say that any day, as it looks like humans are always trying to kill each other off. Humans are amazing, you know. Survival is the key to continuing, and yet there is so much time and energy spent trying to destroy each other. We spirits are still trying to learn why that is, as it makes no sense from what we observe."

"So journeys continue to try to learn why?"

"As you can see, the answer is right here in front of you as we visit. This is all you need. And yet on earth, you have all you need and can't see the forest for the trees.

"That is why you are part of the wave. Hopefully, you and others can bring some common sense to the humans to teach them the basic values of life. It's right there in front of them. But as easy as it is for spirits to see and enjoy, it is so invisible for humans to see and understand. It's like the cloak of humanism is a built-in blinder to the truth.

"This is a real puzzle for spirits, so we keep trying to learn and teach at the same time. And that is why you are here and participating in the wave. You must continue on your path on this journey. Do not waiver from the task. It is important to be part of the wave. After all, your entire journey was designed and created for this task from the very beginning. I personally participated, as you know. And enjoyed every minute of it too. After all, you have a great family here, as do all others.

"You have the gift of enjoying your family on earth too. And hopefully you can teach others to do the same.

"So it's time for me to get on with my day here and time for you to get back to your assignment.

"I love you as always. May your day be peaceful and productive.

"Love to all."

Annie ... Finding the Soul

Hello and good morning to us all.

I open the door with a specific question, and I am surprised I have not asked it yet. I notice I am back to the original location. The little babbling brook is missing too. I do like the babbling brook. Maybe someday I will have a babbling brook near me where I live. I sure hope so.

There are spirits pouring down from the mountains and enjoying today. They are coming and going in all directions at a casual pace. However, I can see one spirit heading toward me, even though it does seem to be far away. But I have learned there is no distance in the Everywhere, and well, here she comes. Wow.

I say, "Hello, I am Bill."

And she laughs and says, "Good morning, Bill. It is such a great day. I was enjoying my day and got caught up in its peace and tranquility. My name is Eureka. So nice to meet you. But then"—she laughs—"we have met before. You just may not remember."

I am caught off guard. I say, "Nice to meet you, Eureka. You sure did get here quickly, as I saw you heading for me in the distance."

Eureka says, "Now, Bill, there is no distance. I just took in the view on the way, or I could have been here in an instant, you know."

"Okay, Eureka, you have piqued my interest. Where did we meet before?

What was your name?"

She says, "Why? Don't you recognize me?" And she laughs.

"Uh, no." I laugh too. "After all, the cloak is missing. I have no memory as a human, but I am sure I do as a spirit."

Eureka says, "Do you have any feelings of déjà vu? You know, that happens all the time."

I say, "Not sure. Since I have learned about déjà vu, I know I can recognize déjà vu when I think about it. Deja vu only creeps up on me when I don't realize déjà vu is a memory of a past experience. The past being any time before now, and that is a long time."

Eureka says, "Yes, forever is a long time, but I met you in an earlier life but not that long ago, sort of, since there is no time in the Everywhere. Why, it just seems like yesterday."

"Eureka, give me a clue? Please."

"It was in Ireland when you and Susie were there. And I was your neighbor, sort of. I lived on the farm next to you. You were a few years older than me, but I did have a crush on you. You were a handsome sort then, you know. But you and Susie were an item." And she laughed. "You two did make a good couple. Do you have any inkling of Ireland?"

"Well, Susie and I have déjà vu thoughts of Ireland but have not really had any details, at least not me."

"Maybe Susie?"

"Not sure."

"It's nice to see you and Susie back together again. You sure do fit each other."

"Eureka, what was your name back in Ireland?"

She laughs and says, "As soon as I tell you, you probably will have memory. My name was Annie."

And in a flash, everything about Annie came over me. "Eureka, or Annie—I'm not sure what to call you now—I sure have a feeling now that I did know and remember you. Wow, that is amazing. I don't have any details but do sense something. Is that normal?"

She smiles and says, "Yes, it's déjà vu all over again. I can see clearly as a spirit, and when you return some day, you and I will speak of this day and laugh about déjà vu. Susie will also, as I used to sneak around and follow you two. I was so jealous as a teenager, you know. Well, let's just leave it at that for the time being.

"So, I see you are working hard on your part of the wave. How is it going?"

I say, "Fine, I think. I just write what all of you bring to me. After all, I am in a human cloak and kind of limited. I am sure you know what I mean. I am faithfully trying to gather as much information as I can.

"Sometimes I bring questions to the Everywhere, and a spirit or two visits with me, and I have direct responses. I only write what is brought to me and keep me out of the process. I am just the human who is delivering the information, as you know."

Eureka says, "Yes, that's true but really important. After all, it's information that you have received from us that will provide the truth to the humans. It's as if humans are walking in the fog, and the answers are all around them. We spirits are always amazed at this phenomenon and not sure why humans can't see the forest for the trees."

"Well, Eureka, I do have a question. Humans, including me, are curious as to where the soul is located in our bodies. We all know, as humans, what makes up our bodies, and yet no doctor or scientist can see the soul. How can that be?"

Eureka smiles and says, "I was hoping you were going to ask me a tough question, but then I am happy to answer this one, as it is so important to your message.

"Let me ask you. When you first visited the stump at Lily Dale, did you see spirits?"

"Why, no, I did not."

"Yet when Susie took your picture at the stump, we were all around you, right?"

"That is true," I said. "That was an eye-opener for me."

"Well, there is you first clue," Eureka says. "You know, doctors and scientists can gather up all the elements and items that make up a human and look at it all from any which way they wish, and they will not find the soul. And that is because the soul cannot be seen.

"You can evaluate the cloak of humanism any way you wish, and you will not see the soul. That is the beauty of the Everywhere. We are all-knowing, all-powerful, and all-loving. And we wrap ourselves with the cloak of human, an animal, a plant, or whatever we are to be during that journey, and we are invisibly surrounded by that cloak.

"Our soul carries life, and when we decide it's time to remove the cloak, life as you know it does not exist anymore. And that is because the cloak is just a cloak. It had no life before or after our uncloaking.

"Don't think for a second that humanism is the center of the Everywhere, because it is not. The spirits and the Everywhere are just that, everywhere and everything. The human cloaking is just like a dream to a spirit. It is just like our visit in Ireland that I remember vividly right now, and you can only sense it because you are clouded by your human cloaking.

"And you will only fully understand the answer to this question when your journey is complete, just like Susie and all the others. You are cloaked and designed to learn for us. That is your purpose, and it is very important. Humans and all other cloaking are designed to answer and learn everything we did not know before so we can remain all-knowing all the time.

"You are, as a human, very important to each and every spirit because your journeys drive our understanding of the Everywhere and everything. Humans and others are important, as they provide lessons to the spirits. Learning is what everything is all about. Your current cloaking is just as important as your last cloaking in Ireland. All journeys bring specific lessons back to us all.

"Your soul is you and is here, there, and everywhere, just like mine is. Your soul is you without the cloak. It's just as simple as that.

"It may be a challenge for you in human form. But like I said, when you return, with or without déjà vu, you will know your soul instantly, as that is who you are.

"So whether you wish to remember me as Eureka, Annie, or another name, I will see you when you return. Keep doing the good work you do.

"Keep smiling and tell Susie I said hello. Love to you all."

And Eureka-Annie moves on to her day in the Everywhere.

Planetary Travel

Good morning to us all.

Wow. I open the door to a new view today. This is a wooded area with a rather large lake and beach in front of me. You can see mountains all around on the horizon, but there is a path of sorts winding through the woods, and I can see a bench or two in the distance, along with one here by my portal door. This is breathtaking, as the lake has no waves but has a perfectly smooth surface like a mirror. I can see spirits winding along the path and walking across the lake in a way. Never saw that before. But hey, I guess you can when you are a spirit; you do as you like. Today verifies that for sure.

As a matter of fact, one spirit who was with a small group on the lake just turned and is coming directly toward me. It's like the spirit is floating a few feet above the water. There is a relatively steep bank in front of me, and the spirit masters the bank as it just walks or floats right up to me.

"Good morning to you," I say.

The spirit stops in front of me and says, "Yes, it is a good morning. Just look at the beauty of this area. It is just astounding. Hi, my name is Lilly. I thought I would visit today."

I say, "Sure!"

She says, "I am good friends with Pap and your family and thought it would be nice to stop and visit."

"Are you from our family tree here?"

Lilly says, "No, but as you know, our family trees are connected, and everyone knows Pap. He is everyone's friend. Even though we all are, Pap seems to be even more special than most. It's kind of hard to describe Pap, but he is always there for everyone. And yet we don't need anyone here, as it is perfection, but Pap is just that special person that everyone just adores and respects. If anyone here is a leader, I guess you could say your Pap is. But he would never admit it. He says his family is just a plain family like all others. He is amazing."

I said, "My family prides itself on being plain people. We practice that on earth too."

Lilly says, "Well, there is nothing plain about your Pap—that's for sure." She smiles.

"So tell me, Lilly, are you here for a reason? Tell me about Lilly please."

Lilly says, "Well, my last journey was in the mid-1800s during the Civil War. I was just seventeen when the war broke out. Yes, I was a Yankee, as they say. I was from the North, New York state to be exact. Just a small town back then, called Ithaca, named after an Indian tribe, from what I understand.

"Just finishing up high school and being courted by a nice young man named Bobby. We were so in love. He would pick me up, and we'd go for long buggy rides and walk in the woods around a lake most of the time. There are a lot of lakes in New York, you know." And she laughs.

"Anyway, we talked about getting engaged and being married. His family were farmers, and my family ran the general store. So our lives were different in a way. Not sure I wanted to be a farmer, because they really work hard and live in the country. I grew up with everything around me. So we were working through that on our walks a lot. Lots of buggy talk. Every now and then, we would sneak a kiss. But that was pretty out there back then, you know.

"Wow … kissing was great, but the war started, and Bobby was a solid American, as were all others, both North and South. He signed up and went to war. After only a few weeks, I was so heartbroken and missed him so much. The word came out that nurses were needed desperately. So, not thinking about if for long, I signed up with the blessing of my family, and away I went to war myself. I basically traveled behind the Yankee front as they marched to the south. When we got to Virginia, Maryland, Pennsylvania, and the Middle Atlantic states, there was constant fighting and skirmishes almost every day. It amazed me how the North and South of the same country were so divided.

"I saw many soldiers come to our tents all shot up. Limbs missing, as they were many times amputated in the field just to save them and then brought to the tent to heal and recoup. Then they would return home to their families. A wagon left every day with soldiers returning home all bandaged up from their wounds. But there were no bandages for the memories of the war. It was awful.

"Bobby was brought back to our tents eventually, but it was too late for Bobby. He had died in the field fighting. Needless to say, I was devastated. He was the love of my life. But I had no choice. I had to continue my nursing. Those boys needed me." She smiled. "Most every soldier that came to my tent wanted to marry me. They would propose within days of returning. I would smile and say, 'Thanks, and I love you too, but I am a nurse and too busy to think about anything right now.' And I'd give them a smile and hope to get them to the wagon in one piece so they could return home.

"They were so cute, but my Bobby was gone. I loved him so. I was asked by many men to marry after the war, you know. But I never married. No one could replace the buggy rides with my Bobby. I continued nursing and helped many people over the years. Many that I helped were some of the same men I helped in the war. It took its toll on many people after that. It was horrible and such a waste of humanism. War is hell, as they say. I still do not see any reason for war, but there are bad folks out there. Some journeys are just horrific as balance tries to maintain a level of learning, and I guess balance does what balance does. I will be going on a journey soon. I hope balance does its magic. Not wanting to have a journey like that for a while, at least. But I am past due for a journey. Your Pap said to me my last journey was like several journeys all in one. That's why I had so much time off from journeys. He's always so kind and understanding.

"So, in a way, I am looking forward to my next journey. But I sure do love it here."

I say, "This seems to be so different than my normal view when I open the portal. I don't know why."

Lilly says, "Well, in a way, it is. You are in a different part of the Everywhere today." And she smiles.

I say, "I don't understand."

Lilly says, "I know you recently read about the first planet discovered years ago that may have a similar environment as earth."

I say, "Well, as a matter of fact, I did. I read that they estimate the planet was 1,400 light-years away from earth. If I understand that, it would take 1,400 human years traveling at a speed of 186,000 miles per hour per second to get there. That's just not possible. At least I don't think that is possible."

Lilly smiled and said, "Maybe as a human, it may not be possible, but I thought it would be fun to have you visit there today." And she smiles as the look on my face must have been worth it.

I say, "Lilly, are you kidding me?"

Lilly says, "Yes, you are at this very second on that planet, and when you walk through the portal to return to earth, you will leave this beautiful planet behind.

"Remember, the Everywhere is everywhere, and there is no boundary or distance in the Everywhere. And we spirits can be wherever, whenever we wish at any second. Just thought you would like to be a space traveler for once.

"Actually, you have been traveling like this for many walks through the portal, but it was just too early for you to understand.

"There are many planets here in the Everywhere just like this. It's up to you and the wave to teach humans to understand they can visit here or live here if they wish. They just have to learn enough to make it possible. And the learning is right in front of them. Get rid of the power and greed and live by the values you brought with you as a human, and this awaits you. It would be nice for humans to experience this, but when you return from your journey, it's here for you whenever you wish."

"Wow, Susie and I sure would love to see this."

Lilly says, "I understand. And you will. Make sure you have a beautiful and perfect day today.

"May peace be with you. Love to you all."

I walk through the portal, and in a flash, I just traveled 1,400 light-years. What a hoot.

What's in a Name?

Good morning to us all.

I open the portal today, and it is a bit different. Everything seems to be brighter. Not sure, even after all this time, why there is so much light when I see no sun, but hey, that's the way it is in the Everywhere. There is no darkness at all. Seems kind of fitting though.

I look around to see similarities, but there is less small plant life and more trees. There are groves of trees Everywhere. The brook is a bit fuller and seems to be traveling a little faster, as if going downhill. It's like a mini rush of water. The babbling brook is more like a flowing stream today. I have never experienced rain in the Everywhere, so I am not sure where the water comes from. But the Everywhere apparently does not need rainfall to resupply the environment.

I see many spirits today, maybe a bit more than normal. They are not moving as slowly as they have in the past. Everything, everywhere seems to have a bit more jump in the spirit, and I say that with tongue in cheek, of course.

Needless to say, as I observe, I see a spirit wandering toward me, and as if magic has been applied, two stumps appear in front of me, as if they came out of nowhere.

One is a bit larger than the other, and I, with respect, go over and stand by the smaller stump. After all, I am visiting.

The spirit approaches and says, "Good morning, Billy, and how are you today?"

I say, as Pap taught me, "Pretty good," and always add a smile. I think of Pap every time I say that. I smile, as it is a wonderful feeling to know Pap is always with me in spirit.

The spirit says, "Today, my name is Todd." And he looks at me with grace and dignity.

"Todd," I say, "I trust you are having a great day."

He says, "As always, I do."

"Todd," I say, "what brings you to me today, as I have many questions to ask in time, but today, there seems to be no specific question I seek an answer to."

Todd says, "I suspect there is an uneasiness today. Do you feel the uneasiness as I do?"

"Not really, Todd, but I do sense a difference today. Everything seems to be brighter and faster. Does that mean anything to you?"

Todd says, "Well, maybe, but then maybe is always a yes in the Everywhere," and he smiles.

"One thing seems to be popping up today for some reason. It seems so many times when humans think about life or the lack of life as a human, they have lots of questions and concerns. Is there a way to overcome these feelings as a human?"

Todd smiles and says, "Unfortunately not. It is a weakness of humanism as humans just, many times—frankly, most of the time—do not grasp the reality of the Everywhere as compared to the reality of the earth or humanism. The cloak of humanism is so overwhelming but only when cloaked. The power of the human spirit is so strong, and that is why we, as spirits, study and learn so much from humans, although it can be a difficult way to understand so many times.

"Because we learn so much, so many more questions keep arising, almost out of nowhere, if that makes any sense.

"The unclear understanding of humanism as a temporary cloak is always a mystery to so many. They just do not grasp how a human came from nothing, so to speak, how they became a human in the blink of an eye as they cloak up, and then they are surprised or not understanding of leaving the cloak behind. Humanism is so temporary and only for the purpose of learning, yet it is so overpowering as a feeling of normalcy to a human. They do not grasp the power of the Everywhere.

"Yet, to spirits, life on earth as a human is like the snap of a finger to a human in time. Our spirit-ness has been from the beginning, whenever that was. If there was indeed a beginning, we spirits were there, and we will be there forever in the Everywhere. There is no end in the Everywhere, just like there are no edges or ends of the Everywhere.

"The Everywhere is all-inclusive and goes on infinitely in all directions, just like our spirit-ness. Yet a human form, a cloak, for the understanding of humanism, is here and gone in a flash. Humans cling to it for a reason we spirits do not understand. After all, the second you step away, so to speak, from your cloak, you know everything about Everywhere and all its glory and wonder. You have returned to yourself in spirit. You are now home.

"Billy, how can that be so difficult to understand as a human? Yet, we learn each and every time that it is so powerful. Family, love, honor, trust, and peace are all you take with you to humanism and all you bring back. If power and greed were in your life as a human, they do not return. You are you in spirit. And that is all that is, and yet that is all it should be too. This is perfect. Yet so many humans question the beauty of the story, I guess you could say. They are overwhelmed with humanism and cannot grasp the freedom and glory of the spirit. This is so sad, and yet when uncloaking occurs, it is as if a light came on and each human gets it in a flash. We are still amazed by this.

"Billy, look around at all the spirits around you. Can you sense any questions, fears, or sadness from any spirit here? Or ever on your visits?"

"No," I say. "Absolutely not. There is no sense of unknowing or lack of anything. The Everywhere is perfect, as they say. Everything always turns out to be perfect. This is said on earth, and yet, now that I think of it, it is almost taken out of context, as humans think of perfection in human terms, when, in reality, perfection is only as a spirit."

"Perfectly stated," says Todd, and all the spirits laugh at his pun.

"Fear is a human issue," Todd says. "Not sure why humans fear, but it goes with the cloak, as they say. Fear is always studied here in journey after journey. We spirits are amazed at how fear is so powerful for humans and yet so not worthy of an emotion. Fear is a weakness of the human cloaking, as we have tried to understand fear, and yet there is no explanation for this total waste of time as a human. What good does fear do for a human?" Todd asks.

"Actually, Todd, I have fears as a human like others, but when I enter the portal, the fears I have just disappear as if I left fear behind the curtain of the portal. Not sure if that makes any sense. Fear of height, fear of anything in my human form is gone in a flash. And I understand my task while here. It is just to carry the truth back to earth and tell the truth to all as part of the wave. That is my task. I have no talent to add to that. Or to embellish the stories or the lessons. I just deliver the truth of the day, the week, or the month and year. I am just to deliver the mail, and I smile. It's the easiest thing to do, just tell the truth."

"It is up to each human to grasp the truth and accept the truth or live under the veil of fear. Such a waste of time, as I said," says Todd.

"I delivered the mail like this one time on a journey, many journeys ago. And still, even with my message, there are those who still fear and do not believe. Fear is such a waste of time and apparently a waste of my journey, but we all learn when we are cloaked with the weight of humanism." He smiles, as do all the other spirits surrounding our conversation. They all know and understand. This is unusual today, as spirits all around are listening intently to our conversation.

Normally they are all just going about their business. It's like it was the first day of my visits, when everyone was surrounding me and welcoming me to my true assignment with the portal entrance. They all knew then, and now my visits have become a normal part of the day. But today is different.

Todd has attracted many to listen. He apparently has a way like Pap. He knows everyone. But then everyone knows everyone here.

"So tell me, Todd, what did you do as Todd in your journey?"

Todd says, "I had assignments just like you. I had to deliver the mail too. I am no different than all the other spirits here. We all have to learn and help each other learn from our journeys. It is the right thing to do as we continue our question to know all. As Todd, and as all my other journeys, they are all to learn. I did my part and will continue to do so on my next journey, as you will too. As we all will." He looks over those who are attentively listening.

He laughs and says, "We just change our names for the fun of it," and they all laugh.

"Have you thought of your names from your past journeys?" asks Todd.

"No, not really, but I suspect I had crazy and fun names like all of you."

Todd says, "We all have fun names that, many times, we just make up. I chose Todd today because it is just a normal name. Kind of fun to be just Todd too!

"Let's just leave today with a final comment. Teach as many as you can to not fear. It is a human thing to overcome, we all understand here in the Everywhere.

"But fear is only temporary.

"Some fear deep water until they learn to swim. Some fear height until they learn to fly. So don't be fearful of fear.

"Fear is just a feeling. It is not a reality like the Everywhere.

"Enjoy your day. May peace and love be with you. It is a glorious day, even on earth as a human.

"Love to all," and Todd travels on with his day.

Why Fear?

Good morning to us all.

I opened the portal today very carefully because I never know if I am going to be on a cliff, in a desert, or on another planet. I am not afraid, except of heights, as I still can't get over being overwhelmed with the fear of height. I'll blame the cloak. So today is a day of normalcy, I see. Back to the original view with two stumps awaiting. This is a calming feeling.

I have a seat and notice many spirits enjoying the day. They are everywhere, and the spirits are pouring down the mountainsides on the horizon. Sure looks normal to me.

Suddenly a spirit begins heading my way. "Hello," I say as the spirit positions himself on the stump.

"Hello," he says, "I am Orn."

"Well, that is an unusual name," I say.

Orn says, "Yes, that is why I like it. Ever met an Orn before?" He laughs. "Gotcha!"

"I can't say I have. Is this your name from your last journey, or is this just a name you have decided to use for the visit?" I laugh.

"It's my name, and I am sticking with it." We both laugh.

"Orn, tell me about your last journey."

Orn smiles and says, "I never thought you would ask. During my last journey, I belonged to a hidden tribe in the Amazon River basin. My tribe is way back at the mouth of the Amazon. Few outsiders ever visit with us, and that is great. We live off the jungle and fend for our families. Our tribe has been doing this for as long as our previous generations have told us. The stories are passed down among the elders, just like all other families. Nothing new there."

"So tell me, Orn, what is so different about your last journey compared to other journeys on earth at this time?"

Orn smiles and says, "Most of all, my tribe has no idea what they are missing. They love their lives as a tribe, even though it is really difficult at times. There are always dangers in the jungle, but we manage through all for the most part. Sometimes a tribesman loses his cloak and returns to the Everywhere, but our tribe worships and honors the journey, as do others from other cultures and corners of the earth. Death for humans is so much a ritual, and this is always a lesson for all of us who have returned to the Everywhere.

"Spirits are amazed at this tradition or process humans go through. They act like it is an ending, yet most of their religions they practice do not teach of any endings but of returns to heaven or some next journey. Yet humans don't believe themselves, we guess. It is such a puzzle, and we are always trying to learn why. It seems that question is always part of every journey—why? Why do humans not believe in their own teachings? Can you answer this?"

"Well, as you know, religions are just a culture's interpretation or belief that each tribe uses to try to understand life as they know it, and life after as they know it, I guess. But you are correct. On the day of uncloaking or toward the end of journeys for most, the fear of life after humanism is questioned even when they have been taught some type of related lesson for most of their lives as humans."

"This is still a puzzle. Even though most of humans' teachings are pieces and parts of the reality of life, it is still questioned until the realization of the uncloaking. After all, we all have experienced this phenomenon as we uncloak and still do not understand why."

"Orn, maybe part of my assignment in the wave is to try to answer this concern or fear for many."

Orn says, "Well, I hope you do, as humans sure do need some clarity for their journeys and to appreciate their uncloaking. After all, the weaknesses of humanism are over immediately when they uncloak and return to the reality of the Everywhere. Perfection awaits them. Look around. You can't beat perfection."

"How we got there from your tribe is pretty amazing, Orn."

"Well," Orn says, "I have a tendency to run on from time to time. After all, your family tree runs on too, you know."

"I agree. I remember my grandmother sent me a letter when I was living in another state. She was in her eighties and probably had not written many letters, if any, for most of her life. But she felt compelled to write me a letter. It was three pages long and basically one sentence. I loved that letter because Nana was just being herself. She could go on and on, even on paper. What a wonderful memory of my Nana." I pause and can tell Nana is close by and smiling.

"Orn, here we are again. Let's get back to your tribe. What did you learn from your journey?"

"Well, the interesting part, and most obvious, was that not much is different in the jungle than in the middle of a city."

"Orn, now that seems so difficult to understand."

Orn says, "Okay, let's think about that for a second. There are tribes or cultures all over the earth. They all have their own languages and their own beliefs and traditions. And they try to maintain their traditions and beliefs from other cultures, as if trying to protect themselves from others. And yet some of the cultures have been at war with each other for hundreds of years and fighting for the sake of fighting in many circumstances. They war with each other because their ancestors did? Still can't figure that one out. Their cultures are almost identical, and since their ancestors fought, they fight. You could say that about tribes in the east, and you could say that about tribes in your country. Racism, north versus south, it still goes on in its own way. It's different but still the same. Right?"

I say, "You are sadly correct."

Orn continues, "With my tribe in the Amazon, our tribe fights with another tribe on the other side of the river. No one can tell us why, except we have been at odds with them forever, it seems, so I guess we still fight, they say. After all, their tribe did such and such to us decades ago, and we are taught to defend our tribe and continue the feud, so to speak. Crazy as it may seem, it still goes on today.

"No matter how different we try to set up the assignments to learn why, it always remains the same. Humans are still so crazy to follow this phenomenon. Yet in some ways, humans are the same too.

"After all, each of you becomes a human by bringing only the values with you. And the values are always the same. And when you uncloak, you can only bring the values with you, as you know. And everything in between during your cloaking is all over the board, as humans say, but the values are still the only thing that really counts. And humans really can't see the forest for the trees, can they?" And we both laugh.

"So, yes, your wave has its hands full, as humans say. You have your work cut out for you. It seems so difficult, and yet, when you think about it, it is so simple.

"How do humans say—you just have to get back to square one, where you began. Maybe that is what tattoos are really for. Maybe everyone should have that tattooed on their arm so they don't forget." And we both laugh.

"Anyway, we have had a good time today meeting and talking about some lessons even though we ran on a bit. But that's okay, as humans say."

It was a good visit, as usual.

"Make sure you have a great day, Billy. If I was holding a microphone like they do on earth, I would drop the mic and say, 'Orn out,' and go about my day.

"Peace and love to you all." Orn meanders away.

Sudden Uncloaking

Good morning to us all.

I open the portal today and find the home view. It appears that I am in the same view but in a different part. There is a large grove of trees, and the bench is in the middle. I can barely see through the trees, but I have identified the mountains on the horizon and the babbling brook behind me. There is a knoll on the other side of the brook, which looks to be where I normally have my meetings. As they say on earth, close but no cigar.

I almost begin to laugh at myself as I hear a spirit behind me laughing. I turn, and there she is just about to hop on the bench. She says, "Close but no cigar?"

Laughing, she says, "How human is that?"

"Okay, I agree. I still can't get used to spirits knowing my thoughts. It's a bit unnerving." I laugh.

She says, "Not to worry, we are harmless. My name, by the way, is Harriet. Good morning!"

I say, "Harriet, what a wonderful name. It's a name I remember from my past."

She says, "Yes, I know, but that Harriet is a different Harriet. Besides, she is still on earth. You just haven't seen her for quite some time. But she is fine." Harriet laughs. "Let's just say I am an earlier Harriet."

"Okay, earlier Harriet. I do have a question today."

Harriet says, "Fire away."

"Well, just a few days ago, a human was at a state fair where he was enjoying an amusement ride, and there was an accident in which he died instantly. Just such a sad ending, as happens many times.

"His story was so compelling. He was going to graduate from high school soon and was planning to join the service and then become a policeman. He was loved and respected by all who knew him. And then, with such a great future ahead of him, poof, his journey was over.

"Now, I know this journey, like all journeys, was planned. But what lessons did he provide to the spirits?"

"Oh my," Harriet says. "So many lessons. He was a remarkable young human, as you know. And his journey will affect many humans around him, including those who did not know him. His lesson, or at least his main assignment, was to provide lessons to learn for many other humans. Just imagine how his sudden uncloaking has made many around him learn how to react to these unplanned, sudden uncloakings. His memory will live on in many humans for the rest of their journeys. His memory will change dozens as to how they live their lives and what decisions they make on their journeys.

"His life as a human was not wasted but was invested in so many other humans. He, like you, is part of the wave. He will leave nothing but great thoughts of values, and he provides strong messages even to those who did not know him. For his journey was full of values. He leaves with all he came with, and many will have learned this.

"Because, to many who were close to him, he had already taught them that the values he had was all he needed to be happy and excited about his life and his plans. He had no regrets and lived each day as if it were his last. And then it was.

"Sad to say, his uncloaking came early to most, but it was on time for his assignment. There is no reason to be sad, but there are plenty of reasons to honor his presence as a human. He taught so many while on earth. His part of the wave was well delivered. And he is proud to have served his journey with such success.

"His memory will now live on in the lives of others. They have all been permanently affected by his presence. What an honor for him."

"Wow, thank you. I hear of these journeys that end so suddenly for many, and at first, it is so sad, but in the grand plan of the Everywhere, lessons are learned for others to learn and for spirits to learn too.

"All is perfect. And all who served on their journeys are rewarded with their return to the Everywhere. Perfection is ahead for each who serve their journeys with lessons."

"Exactly," Harriet says. "It is sad for humans but joyful for spirits and for the human who completed their journey to return to the Everywhere where they belong.

"It's beautiful and fulfilling for us all.

"You are living proof of how each human will affect others. Your journey, with still much to do, will and has affected many in your own way already. Each human fulfills the lessons they are to provide. That's the beauty of the journey.

"They are all to be the way they are, and they will provide lessons to others."

"So, Harriet, tell me about the lessons you provided on your journey."

Harriet says, "Well, I'll be honored to do so. I was born to be a Yankee," and she laughs. She says, "Let me start again," as she composes herself. "I was born in what you call New England. Most humans don't even think of it like this, but back then, New England was named in honor of where many humans originally called home, England. And little did they know then that England would become their enemy of sorts, at least for a while. We all know how the Revolutionary War came and went.

"And now New England was the section of America that was only a mention in history. Now, many years later, people refer to New England as a region of the US with little recognition of its original nickname.

"Anyway, I digress. Years later, I was born to a family of the local general store. Our store was the center of activity in our small town. Everyone gathered there for supplies and the local news, as our store had the news before it made it to the local newspaper. Yes, rumors flew back then just as they do today. But with all the rumors came the truth too.

"I was still in school when the war broke out between the Yankees and the Rebels. Yes, the Civil War. It was a horrible time in history, as we all know. But at the same time, I guess it was necessary. Power and greed had overtaken many, and lives were being ruined, and lessons were being learned. It was time for action, and a wave of sorts began. The Yankees responded, and the great Civil War erupted.

"I, being a female, was told I could not fight. It was not ladylike to even think of doing that. It was for the men to take care of, I was told. Well, frankly, that infuriated me. I was no different than males when it came to principles and the practice of values. After all, I had my lessons to teach too, you know. So, I announced to my family I was going to join the army and fight too. Well, that was not to happen, so to speak. Not according to my father. He did have the last say, you know. Well not really." She laughed.

"Needless to say, I was not happy. And I was not going to let my father's ruling be so final. For the next few nights, I pondered and prayed for a way to be a Yankee like all others. And then it came to me.

"The next morning at the breakfast table, I announced to my family I was going off to the war to be a nurse for the soldiers. I was going to do my part.

"My father was upset but not angry. He was upset because he knew that was what I had to do, as it was my journey to do so. Even though he did not fully understand things back then, he knew in his heart it was the right thing for me to do. He agreed with my plan and supported my decision. He knew nurses would be needed.

"So off to the war I went. I took a train to Philadelphia, and that is where I joined the nurses, and they taught me all I needed to know to get started. I guess you could say we learned as we went to war. I did not expect to be so close to the front lines. We could hear the shots of war constantly. Our days were full of strife and trauma. It was horrible. And our nights were full of tears as we tried to rest for what was to happen tomorrow.

"I was not alone, as all of us suffered along with the soldiers. It was as if we were there with them. But our need as nurses was overwhelming. And for me, I could not stop. I was there when they needed me, and I saw things that no one should see and experience. But nurses had no choice. After all, many times we were the last person a soldier would see before they uncloaked to the Everywhere. I still can see their eyes as they uncloaked. It was so sad, and yet I loved every one of them for their sacrifice.

"They were doing what they believed in, no matter what the results were to be. I, too, believed in the cause. We fought the same war, and eventually, this horrific challenge was over.

"I returned to my little town in New England a changed woman. I was happy to be alive and happy to return. But I returned with a burden. I could not speak of the horrors of war. It was too hurtful to do. But I lived a life of serving. After all, I was a nurse. And frankly, a good one. I worked in the local hospital for the rest of my working life. I helped all I could, but the hospital was different. It did not include war, so it was much better. But many times, old soldiers would come to the hospital with old wounds of war they could not overcome. The strife of the war came with them. War changes you. And war teaches you too.

"It was meant to be. And in our own way, we all came home with lessons, even though most of us could not speak of war. But our actions were the results of war, and we lived and taught others in so many ways.

"War is evil, but sometimes war is war, and it is to be. My life was long and full. I did marry eventually, but it was too late for children for me. But I was an aunt to others, and they were my children, so to speak.

"I lived through my nieces and nephews and my family. They were my anchor. They were my family. I lived by the values I came with, and I proudly returned to the Everywhere, lessons in hand and fulfilled by my efforts.

"After all, I was a nurse. I was a Yankee. I did my part.

"And now I am back in the Everywhere, happy and ready for my next journey.

"Billy, I hope I helped you today with my journey. We all have lessons to teach. Just like the young man who uncloaked at the fair. He is here now and proud of his journey and the assignments he carried out.

"You must tell our story. You must tell of the values. You must make the wave do its work. I wish you well, and may peace and love be part of your day today."

And Harriet is off to the woods to enjoy her day.

Making Decisions

Good morning to us all.

I open the portal today to a really neat and different view. I am in the middle of what appears to be a huge meadow with grasses as tall as I am. There are mountains around me in all directions, and yes, there are spirits pouring down the mountains. But the grass is so tall I cannot see the bottom. However, there is a well-worn path I am standing in. Except for the mountains, this is all I can see. So I will work my way along the path to find whatever comes to light.

But what direction do I take? Now *that* is the question of the day. Which way do I go? It's a big decision. Well, I think I will go to my right. No real reason; maybe it is the right way.

As I wander down the path, and apparently in just a few steps, I see I have made the right decision. There is a round clearing, with a bench and a spirit waiting for me.

I say, "Good morning! I am glad I made the right decision."

She laughs and says, "I knew you would. My name is Fola, and I bring you this peaceful and beautiful day today."

"Nice to meet you. Fola. Tell me, what would have happened if I went the other direction?"

Fola laughs and says, "I guess we will never know. You decided, as you have many times. Sometimes humans make the right move, and others, well not so much.

"Life is all about making decisions. And every time a human has to make one, they have at least two choices. And that's why we learn so much from humans." She pauses for me to gather that thought and wade through it.

I say, "Now that you bring that up, we have decisions to make all the time. Maybe not so many big decisions, like buying a home or who to marry, but we have decisions to make."

Fola says, "Journeys change with every decision. We just keep learning and learning. Decisions are like fingerprints. They are all different. Each journey has its own beginning and ending and so many decisions in between."

"I never thought of it like that before, but you are so right."

Fola says, "Is that why you made the decision to go right today instead of left?" We both laugh.

"Would I have met you if I went the other direction?"

Fola says, "Well, you will never know. So maybe it was a bigger decision than you think. Maybe the little decisions you make in life are bigger than you think too."

"I don't understand, Fola. What do you mean?"

Fola says, "Every time a human decides to go left or right, they meet different humans who can change their journey. It's like coming to a crossroad. Every change of direction is a new crossroad, and a journey changes after each one. It's like a giant maze of life every day."

I say, "Fola, you are making me paranoid."

Fola says, "I don't mean to make you feel that way, but in reality, that is the way spirits learn. We allow you to make those decisions on your journey. We quietly know and, in a way, guide you because of your assignments. But many times, you can stay within your assignments and go in different directions.

"As you know, your assignment is to teach others about the Everywhere.

"Since you have no experience, how do you determine what to do and which way to go? Do you blindly go forward and let decisions be made for your assignment, or do you carefully decide your way by looking for signs to assist?"

"Fola, this is getting more difficult every step of the way. What are you suggesting I do?"

"You have those around you who will assist. You and Susie must follow the signs and make the right decision. Each decision will determine the magnitude of your achievement. Yes, every decision is important on earth. It will change your life and those of others if you make the right decision."

"Wow, it appears a big crossroad lies ahead for me."

"Yes, it does, for you and the wave. You have been blessed with many visits to tell others. Lots of lessons are there for humans to learn and, yes, make decisions.

"Your decisions can and will affect other decisions.

"Your journey has a big crossroad ahead. And it is made by many smaller decisions along the way."

"That's a lot to think about. At least for me. I am sure Susie and I will find a way. Tell me, Fola, about your journey."

"I was born to a simple family. My father worked in a quarry, and my mother worked in a laundry. We did not have much, but we did have each other. I had one sister, and we were best friends most of the time." She laughs.

"But life was simple. My father always said, 'We work hard and we play hard.' I am sure you have heard that one before. When my family was not working, we camped and went on mini journeys as a family. We were always on the go. Yet our decisions were always based on simple decisions. We had to have the funds to travel, so in all reality, we traveled cheaply when we could. And camping was the best way we could stretch our assets, as they say.

"But during all those fun little journeys, my parents always took the time to talk with us. My sister, Meli, and I were always learning. And yet it always seemed like there was something more for us to learn after each campsite chat.

"I grew up always wanting to learn more. I went on to college locally, as traveling would use up the assets, you know. We were taught to make logical decisions, but we were also taught how important each decision became in our journey.

"I decided to become a psychologist. How about that? Me, a psychologist.

"And you know what? Even after all that time and education, my time as a psychologist was about teaching my patients to understand the importance of making good decisions. For those I helped, they learned to slow down at each crossroad and think through the simplicity of making the right decision.

"They learned that each decision, each direction taken, will change the course of their life. I helped many along the way. And for others, I tried, and oh how I tried, yet they kept making decisions that complicated their journeys. I had many wins and not so many losses, as we would say, but my journey was full, and I know I made a difference for many.

"And you know, that's all you can do. Just doing your best and making as many right decisions is what a journey is all about.

"And part of my journey was to prepare for today, you know.

"My last chapter on this journey was to meet with you today and tell you my story. How about that? I just uncloaked, and here I am finishing up my journey.

"I spent my lifetime preparing for this moment. And it was worth every moment of time on earth. For today is about making the right decisions for you today and for others who follow this advice.

"Each decision, whether a big decision or not, for that given moment in time, is a big decision.

"I am now complete with my journey. I just came down the mountain over there, and here I am at the famous bench. I now can follow the path here to check in with my family tree and go about my way in the Everywhere. It's like taking a big breath and finishing a big task. And now I can enjoy myself since I am back where I belong.

"My decisions brought me back here, fulfilling my assignment.

"Make sure you have a wonderful and loving day full of good and right decisions." And off on the path she goes.

Bunny and Hunter

Good morning to us all.

I open the portal today and find myself in a different view again.

This time, I am at the foothills of many mountains, as if surrounded. There appears to be a small valley where I am located, and as I look to my right and my left, I see the mountains begin to slowly climb to their peaks. They are not tall, snow-capped mountains like in many pictures but are smaller mountains with trees. They are mostly green, but I can see hints of fall. Wherever I am, there must be seasons of some sort. If this is not earth, and it probably is not, seasons must be part of their Everywhere too.

But then something is so natural about seasons.

After all, there is a birth in the spring, then the glory of the summer, then the changing of the fall, and finally the end in the winter. Kind of like a journey of sorts for plants each year.

It's like the cycle of life each year subtly reminds us about our journeys as humans and other animal life. It's right there in front of us. And yet for many, we do not stop and think about the message.

I begin to look around locally now, and yes, spirits are all about.

And yes, I find my bench. I have a seat and relax, wondering why there is no stump today. After all, stumps would have fit in here more naturally, and I laugh at myself for thinking of the stumps.

Suddenly a spirit comes from behind the bench and surprises me. I laugh at the suddenness of its appearance. "You surprised me," I say.

The spirit says, "Good morning, Billy. Why would you be surprised? You knew a spirit would be here today."

I laugh and say, "I know. I just got caught up in the moment watching all the beauty."

She laughs and says, "I am Meredith, but everyone calls me Bunny."

I say, "What a fun nickname. How did you get that nickname?"

"Well, when I was very young, the first two teeth I earned were my top two teeth, and they were alone for the longest time. So my family all laughingly said I was their bunny, and that's how I got my nickname. And it stuck with me throughout my journey."

"Wasn't it a bit unusual for you to be called Bunny as an adult?"

"Well, those who were acquaintances called me Meredith, and that was fine. But it did not take anyone too long to pick up my nickname, as everyone around me called me Bunny. So it was natural, and well, it just kept happening.

"It had its benefits though. Humans have a tendency to remember unusual things more than normal things. It was easy to remember to most. My name was like a business card of sorts. People recognized me so easily. It was so natural to be walking down the street and hear, 'Good morning, Bunny. Hope you are having a great day!' That's how most of my days would go. So, having Bunny as my name always made humans smile and brightened their day. I was blessed with a great nickname."

"So, Bunny, tell me about your journey."

Bunny smiles and says, "Well, you already know the cornerstone of my journey. I had a great journey and knew from the beginning that I would be treated special in my journey.

"Everyone was always in a good mood around their Bunny." She laughs. "I made friends so easily. I could just be me and did not have to go the extra mile to get attention of others.

"I had a wonderful childhood and school years. I was loved by everyone, and you know, when you are loved by everyone, it is natural to love them back. The values teach this, you know. The values were with me always. I went on to college with the blessing of my parents. I was not looking for a husband, as was the case for many females back then. It used to really bother me when I would hear someone mention that to me.

"I digress … So, I went on to college to learn and earn, as I would say. I wanted to be a businesswoman in a man's world. Back in my generation, that was unheard of. But not for me. I was headstrong and ready for more.

"So I started a marketing company. And back then, most did not really understand what marketing was about, so they would listen to me.

"I made great strides for women in business.

"And then, one day, it hit me: why can't women vote? Well, you know, that really grated on me. So I joined a movement of women who pushed for change. After all, I was the perfect member for this. I was setting new directions for women, so why not? Right?

"Well, at first, my involvement actually hurt my business. There were men who were against women voting. And when they found out I was active in the movement, well ... they backed off a bit.

"But I learned from that. I soon learned that power and greed had hidden agendas. That was a hard lesson. I was a suffragette. One of the first. We were vocal and determined. And you know women now vote and have standing in all decision-making in today's world.

"I am very proud of that. Once that movement was successful and the inevitable presence of women in business arose, I was able to get back to my marketing business and thrive. Now everyone wanted Bunny in their corner.

"So, I had a great life, and yes, I eventually married. But only to someone who I learned supported women voting. He was a good guy. And ironically, his name was Hunter. And everyone had a lot of fun with our names. You can fill in the blanks on that." She laughs.

"I joined in on that one. We had three children, and yes, all three were females. They grew up strong spirited and very successful. Amy was a banker, Aggie owned and managed a hardware store, and Annie was a high school principal. They were all leaders in their fields."

"Why did you name them all with the letter A? Any reason?"

"Yes, of course. Back then, seating in schools was assigned alphabetically, so my daughters all sat in the front. They were able to avoid being caught up in the stuff that happens in the back of a classroom and were great students because of it. My daughters did not take a back seat to anyone.

"So when my seasons were almost complete and it was time for me to return to the Everywhere, my family was around me, along with many of my friends. I was blessed with the thought of when I was young and given the nickname Bunny. How it changed my life.

"It is so important for humans to give their children every opportunity to be successful, and starting with a good name is the first step. My name was surrounded with values, and I lived the life full of values. It made humans accept me and then judge me fairly on my abilities, heart, and values. That's all I needed to be successful, even in the days when women did not have equal opportunities.

"So the values were a natural to me, just like my nickname. I hope the lessons I bring to the bench today can be used.

"Humans get lost in the minutiae so much. We have to create a clear path for the values to stay in place alongside of our souls when cloaked. I can't tell you how important that was for me. So simple yet so difficult for many.

"I hope this lesson helps you with the wave. After all, I was one of the first in the wave and really proud of it too.

"So keep up the good work and tell my story. And make sure everyone gets my message. Keep it simple, especially your name.

"Don't complicate the simplicity of the values and how easy it is to love and be loved. Honor your family by carrying the message.

"Be safe, enjoy your day, and make sure you have love and peace today and every day." And she politely and boldly goes off into the woods on a new venture.

Jake's Deer Company

Good morning to us all.

I open the portal today, and the view is quite different.

I appear to be on a snowcap of sorts. It is crunching under my feet. I remember those days when I was young and it was fun to walk in the snow. There is snow everywhere. It's so beautiful after a fresh snow. All the tree limbs are slightly weighted down, and it's almost majestic.

I just realized that the snow, even though just freshly fallen, is still here even though the temperature is perfect. How can that be?

I look around, and the bench appears behind me. It apparently has just arrived, as it is snow-free.

Well, that is a convenience. I laugh. I have a seat and can see many spirits glowing among the trees. Although I thought the snow would have made it difficult to see spirits because of all the whiteness of the snow, they appear clearly as the orbs pick up a glow that is not as prevalent in other views.

And then I see one glow coming toward the bench. I notice he is coming quickly, with a light bounce in his gate. He arrives and says, "Well, good morning to you, Billy. How is this for a surprise?" and he hops onto the bench.

"Surprised? Yes, this is beautiful. But what surprises me more is the temperature. How can this be?"

He says, "Well, first of all, my name is Jake, short for Jacob. Now, let me explain. I love the snow. On my journey, I lived in the north, and the snow was everywhere most of the year. It was beautiful and wonderful to see. My only dislike for snow was all the cold that came with it. And when I was just a little Jake, I said to my mother, 'Someday I want the snow without the cold.' She said, 'Jake, someday when you are older, find a way for that to happen and make it work for you.' And she laughed and gave me a big hug and a kiss on the cheek. I promised my mom that day that I would. So today, I did just that.

"It's a great day today with snow all around, and the cold is not along for the ride, as they say on earth. Well, I have done this before since uncloaking, so don't let today's effort go to your head." He laughs. I join in.

"I must say, the snow is beautiful, and it's frankly great to be here with the perfect temperature. Just how did you do that?"

"Silly Billy," he says, "I can because I can. Everything in the Everywhere is perfect. So wishing for snow today with a perfect temperature is an easy ask, because it is perfect."

"Well, okay then. Thank you. This is great." We sit for a minute to enjoy the view.

"So, Jake, do you have any special message for me today?"

"Well, I picked up on your question just before I got to the bench. You are curious if a human, just before uncloaking, has a desire to have last moments with loved ones?"

"Is that normal?"

"Well, for humans, it's about the moment. Time is not present here, as you know, but for humans, well, that is a different story. Many times, humans wish to have a last moment with their families. You are correct. But for others who are on the verge of uncloaking and understand how life really is … well, they often prefer to uncloak alone.

"That happens quite often you know. When humans are feeling the love from the Everywhere inviting them to return, the transition from human to spirit by uncloaking is like losing the weight off your shoulders as a human, and the process is quite invigorating in a way.

"Let me explain. When there is a lot of suffering, for example, spirits go to that human and encourage them to complete the uncloaking so they can lose the suffering. Once that connection is made, and the human realizes the last second of fear is behind them, they uncloak as fast as they can, because they want to relieve themselves of the cloak and feel free again. It's an overwhelming and wonderful process, you know.

"So the idea of 'last words' is really a misunderstanding about what is to really happen. They are not the last words. Ever go to a human's funeral and feel uplifted with happiness because everyone is enjoying the memories of the past? Of course, the spirit is visiting with everyone and assuring all is well. It's a wonderful experience for all. Hopefully, it is reassuring to all that all is well, and the uncloaking is as natural as being a spirit again was to be.

"After all, the spirit was just on a journey, you know. So they were just returning to their true home, the Everywhere."

"So, Jake, tell me about your journey."

"Well, I was a young boy from the north, as I mentioned. I love the snow. I lived in the snow. I went to school in the snow. I played in the snow. There always seemed to be snow, except for just a bit of time in the summer. And because there was such a short time, we spent our summers preparing for the winter. We grew foods to store for the winter. We repaired equipment and sleds and sleighs and such. We actually worked very hard preparing for the winter. We all loved the winter but had to prepare for the cold of the winter. It was a way of life in the north country.

"So I grew up wanting to stay, and yet I had to find something that I could do to earn a living. My family were farmers of a sort. They had a dairy farm, and our milk was used to make cheese and other things, of course. But I was not in love with dairy farming. It's an honorable thing to do, and you are always around nature, and I loved that, but I wanted something else to do.

"So in my late teens, it came to me. We went to a farm sale and bought some deer for our sleigh. Up north, it was difficult to make ends meet. So horses were a luxury to most. And they were a luxury to my family too. We had two horses once when I was little, and they suffered and struggled in the snow. They worked hard, and it was great to have two horses, but none of us enjoyed their suffering in the cold. Horses were not to be in this much snow, I think.

"So, most used deer that we caught and trained. And that's where I got the idea. Catching deer was hard work. You had to be in the snow of course, and you had to be fleet of foot to do so. I had a pretty speedy deer that my father gave me. So I would go north and lasso a deer or two from time to time. And when I realized I could have a business of catching and training deer, well that was the answer for me. So I started the Jake's Deer company.

"I was very successful. I had plenty of business to keep my company going and provide for my family. I had a knack for doing so, as I always found the fastest deer to keep as my own, so my job was always easy. I rewarded my own deer after they helped me by selling them to wonderful families that I knew would take good care of them.

"You really get attached to your deer. You know, they are a special animal. Each has its own personality, and it was always fun naming them." He laughs. "My family loved the deer. They helped me on our deer farm, and eventually, I got the idea of having my own deer farm instead of struggling in the cold north winds to catch them.

"So I caught more than my requests for trained deer and began my own herd. And life for me as a deer trainer was wonderful. I could keep my herd warm and healthy and train them. I made good decisions for me and the deer.

"My family was very happy and well taken care of. I eventually got too old to train, and my two sons took care of the deer training for me. After all, I had my bruises and injuries from my younger years to contend with. The body began to give out, and I was harnessed to a wheelchair after years of freedom.

"My human body was done, and the pain was pretty steep. But I never lost my attitude about life. I kept my pain to myself. Being human became a burden. But I loved my family and still wanted to be part of the human journey. I still did not fully understand what was going to happen sooner or later. Then one day, I had an accident and fell out of my wheelchair and went into a coma.

"I could hear a bit, but I was introduced to the transition to spirit at that time. I had a few close calls during that time in a coma. But I still hung on and did not know why. I could hear my family speak to me, and I yearned to get better, but I was drawn to the Everywhere because I sensed a painless, perfect life ahead. And when I realized I could have both and visit when I wished, well, that was it for me. I easily uncloaked and enjoyed my family whenever I wished. Hey, just like your Pap. Make sense now?"

"Yes, it does. I now understand."

"So I promised my mother I would change the cold days of snow with great days of snow, and here we are. I keep my promises." He laughs. "I have days like this quite often, you know. Anytime I wish to, because I can. I visit my family when I wish, because I can. I am free of pain and anguish of the cloak I carried and don't miss it for a second. I have all I ever wanted here. It is perfect in every way. And the snow is here with me too.

"Make sure you have a perfect day today, or at least as perfect as you can make it. Perfection lies ahead for all of you. Enjoy. May peace be with you. Love to all."

Never Give Up

Good morning to us all.

I open the portal today to the home view. The bench is not available today, as the two old familiar stumps are in place. I wonder why the change from day to day. In the midst of everything, I seem to think it's just a matter of the day maybe. A good question, I expect.

I look around, and all seems to be just a normal day. But what is normal in the Everywhere? Another good question.

There are spirits all about today. They seem to be going about their day as if I am just part of the landscaping. I have noticed sometimes it seems spirits are giving me space as they avoid my bench. Having been here so often, I guess I have become part of the landscape.

A spirit along the brook suddenly turns and heads my way. As expected, she is here in a flash and on one of the stumps waiting for me. I laugh and have a seat. "Good morning," I say. "How are you?"

She says, "Well, I am wonderful, thank you. My name is Maddie, short for Madeline."

"I love your name, Maddie. Were you always nicknamed Maddie?"

She laughs. "Yes, from the very beginning when I was just a baby. I had this formal name only used officially, and yet no one ever called me Madeline. Well, now that I think of it, my mother called me Madeline when I was bad—you know, to get my attention."

"Did it work?"

"Well, maybe for a bit, but no, not really."

"So, quick question, Maddie. Why the stumps today and not the bench?"

Maddie says, "Simple answer. You can blame me for the stumps. I am a friend of nature, and I chose the stumps today, as I always do. You don't like the stumps?"

"No, I don't mind the stumps. Just curious and always full of questions."

Maddie says, "Well, the stumps to me are perfect in a perfect world here in the Everywhere."

"Maddie, do you have a new lesson for me today?"

"Well, yes, my lesson comes from my last journey, if that's okay."

"Of course, Maddie. Tell me of your journey."

"I was born to a very poor family. My mother did chores for whoever she could, and my father, well, he was not the most ambitious one, but he would find work from time to time. So it was just me and my parents. I unfortunately did not have any brothers and sisters. We lived outside of a small village along a stone wall. Not much around, just a shack of sorts that we kept trying to keep repaired. It was never-ending. The roof was always leaking, and my father was always looking to fix it when he had the time.

"They both loved me very much and wished for me to be happy. But happy for me was only if my parents were happy, and that just did not seem to be often.

"So, where we lived, it seemed like nothing grew. It was like living on a gravel mound, if you can imagine. There were no trees nearby. It was as if the land surrounding our house was only there for a shack to have a home. Kind of sad in a way. But no one would bother us living like that since we were separated from nature and all around us.

"I loved nature and walked to school every day. I had some friends at school but not many. Most stayed away from me because their parents said I lived on the other side of the tracks, whatever that meant.

"I think it had something to do with my parents. They never had a school to go to when they were children. I knew little of their past, but they did tell me they did not have the chance to go to school, which is why they wanted me to never miss a day. And you know, I didn't.

"I walked to school every day when I was young. There was a store I would walk by that had everything you can imagine. We called it a general store. Not sure why, but it was wonderful. I would stop there almost every day on the way home from school. The owner, Mr. Thomas, was a nice man. He allowed me to stop and visit with him. It was a nice place for me to break up my walk home. I told him one day that nothing would grow near my home, and I could tell he was saddened by that.

"So, life for me when I was young was all about school. My day was always planned around my walk to and from school, and I tried to learn as much as I could. My mother told me it was a way to a new life for me. It was the answer. So I kept looking for the answer.

"Then one day, Mr. Thomas, came up to me while I sat on his porch and said, 'I have something for you.' And he opened my hand and put a seed in my palm. He said, 'You take that home, and you plant it someplace you would like to see it grow.'

"You know, that was the first time anyone ever gave me something.

"So I rushed home, and I had the most difficult time determining where to plant it. There was all this gravel and no dirt. So I went to the very edge of the gravel, which my dad says was our boundary, and I carefully placed it under the gravel. I added water like Mr. Thomas suggested.

"And nothing happened. It just sat there. I watched the rest of the day, and nothing happened.

"The next day, I stopped by to see Mr. Thomas and told him what happened. I was so sad. Mr. Thomas smiled and said all will be fine and not to give up on my plant. He then gave me another seed, and I ran home to plant it next to the other.

"This went on for what seemed to be forever. Every day, I would stop by and visit with Mr. Thomas, and he would give me another seed. I would rush home and plant it and look for the seeds to grow. I had a winding row of seeds buried in the gravel. And still nothing happened.

"Years went by, and still nothing. Mr. Thomas said every day, 'Don't give up. Keep planting. Sooner or later, all your hard work will pay off.'

"I continued every day. And then I came to a time in my life when I was to graduate from school. I had made my parents proud. I had not missed a day.

"I had learned a lot. But what I learned most of all was to never give up. I learned and learned, and actually, my life wrapped around learning and planting a seed.

"Well, I had learned much, but I still had no plants. Mr. Thomas kept telling me to never give up. So all these years, I never gave up on my seeds.

"So the big day came. I had no special clothes to wear. But that was okay. My parents said, 'You go and graduate. We will be here for you when you return.'

"They stayed behind as they always did. I think they did not want to embarrass me with their presence. I was saddened by that, but I understood how they felt.

"There were some fellow students who treated me that way too. After all, I lived on the other side of the tracks. So, on the way to school, I stopped by to see Mr. Thomas, and he was so glad to see me. He had a gift for me, all wrapped up, as if he knew I would stop. And maybe he knew all along. I will never know.

"I asked, 'Why are you giving me this gift?'

"Mr. Thomas said, 'You never gave up you know. Every day, you stopped by, and you always had a great attitude and never gave up. Even though the seeds did not grow, you never gave up.' I opened the box, and there was a new dress and shoes for me. I was so surprised I began to cry. Mr. Thomas was my friend and always was the highlight of my day, and now he gave me a dress to graduate.

"I proudly went to a back room and put on the dress and shoes and came back to show Mr. Thomas. He was all smiles. And he said, 'You look beautiful.' No one had ever said that about me.

"So I went off to graduation. And when I arrived, well, me in a new dress? It was amazing. It's as if everyone noticed me for the first time. It was my reward for never giving up, just like Mr. Thomas said. I enjoyed the day and ran back to the store to tell Mr. Thomas all about it.

"Then he asked me, 'Okay, now what are you going to do?' I stopped and suddenly realized I would not be walking to school anymore and would not be there at the store anymore. I began to cry.

"Mr. Thomas comforted me. He smiled and said, 'Well, now that you are a graduate, you need a job, right?'

"I gathered myself and said, 'What I am going to do?'

"Mr. Thomas said, 'You are going to help me here at the store. I need an employee, you know.'

"Needless to say, I was elated. I hugged Mr. Thomas and ran home to tell my parents of my good news. And when I got the shack, all the plants were popping out of the gravel. They were finally beginning to grow. I never gave up on those seeds, and finally they were rewarding me for being faithful to Mr. Thomas and to my seeds. My parents were elated as to all that happened that day.

"I finally left the store years later after Mr. Thomas uncloaked. But all that time, I always told everyone not to give up on anything. Dreams can come true no matter who you are. You just have to have faith and love for all you do.

"I went on to become a teacher later in life, and I would sit with my first graders and tell all my stories about when I was little. I guess you could say I learned from Mr. Thomas.

"Each and every day, I would give each of my students a seed to take home and plant in their yards and gardens. And you know what? That little village became the most beautiful village of them all.

"Maddie made a difference from that little shack on the gravel. And each one of my students learned of Maddie and carried the message of Maddie on in their lives.

"I did my part for the wave. I uncloaked years later, and when I did, everyone came with a flower from their gardens. I had made a difference because I never gave up.

"And you must do the same. No matter what, do not give up. Make sure you visit each and every day. And make sure you give a seed to everyone to learn every day too.

"May peace and love be with you." And off to the brook she goes.

Everyone Has Talent

Good morning to us all.

I open the portal today to a different view. I am on top of a very high mountain. And yes, I am afraid of heights, but this seems to be a bit different. There is no cliff nearby but a long, steep decline down the side. The mountainside is dotted again with colors of the fall. It is beautiful. The mountain connects to a large valley below, with a range along to my left and right. But the valley seems to go on forever, as I can see a great distance from here.

A narrow creek leads from the base of the mountain and winds its way across the valley to a distant body of water that I can barely make out. I cannot tell if it's an ocean or an extremely large lake.

Spirits are all about as they are making their way down the mountain, and I notice one spirit working his way along the mountaintop to me. I find the two stumps and take a seat, awaiting his arrival.

"Good morning," he says. "I trust you are enjoying this view?"

"I am," I say. "How are you?"

He says, "This is a great day today. It's just perfect. My name is Fritz. And Pap says hello, by the way. As you would expect, he is busy but thinks of you every day."

I say, "I know he does."

"He is enjoying your journey as much as you do."

"Well, with that, I do have a question, Fritz."

Fritz says, "Fire away. I have all the answers, you know."

"Okay, here it is. Can spirits see into the future?"

Fritz is silent. And finally, Fritz says, "Well, yes, we can. After all, we are all-powerful and can do anything, but why would we want to look ahead into the future?"

"Fritz, wouldn't it be great to tell me if my work is successful or not? And if the wave was successful or not? And if journeys are fulfilling or not?"

Fritz says, "Well, we could, but what good would it do? What could be accomplished by such discussion?"

I pause because I can't find the answer. Fritz then says, "See, you already know the answer. It would take away all the learning needed to create a future. That would almost be sacrilegious, don't you think?"

I acknowledge that he is right.

Fritz says, "I know I am. Yes, we can look into the future, but no spirit does for that reason. Spirits are to learn, and we already know it would not be right to do so. We need to learn the details of every action and every reaction to learn and be all-knowing.

"Looking into the future would only distort the journeys involved. On occasion, we come up with what it's like traveling to another planet and the issues needed to overcome to do so. That's really important to almost create goals to plan. But we won't give away what happens. We like the process of the surprise. Besides, earning the way is always best. Learning is always best. Finding your future is what journeys are all about. Don't you think?"

"Well, yes, you are right. I guess that was just my humanism coming out." I laugh as Fritz joins in.

"Fritz, tell me of your journey."

"Well, my journey was full of irony. As you know, I have been on so many journeys and learned a lot. I had always done my part. This time, not sure why or how, but it was different. I grew up in mountains like this. My family were craftsman and artisans. They made clocks and carvings and woodworking of great detail. My father made cuckoo clocks and was known throughout the valley. My mother was a quilt maker and taught others to do the same. She was so graceful with her ways. We had many friends, as our family always brought great joy to those we met and were friends with.

"So I was one of the lucky ones who grew up happy and free. As long as I followed the teachings of my parents, all was well. My father always spoke of tough love when he had to discipline me when younger. I guess I was a handful, as my mother would say.

"I had no interest in cuckoo clocks or quilt making. However, I did like to ski. That was always fun. So I was always looking for something to do that did not require work. I guess you could say I was lazy, but in reality, I was not. I just wanted to do what I wanted to do to have fun and not be responsible. Now that I think about it, my mother was right. I was a handful. So I managed to stay focused enough to make it through school. Just good enough to graduate. My parents were oh so thankful for that.

"What was I to do? I had no skills. I did not like to be responsible. No one would hire me because I could not follow through with anything. I drifted along for a while. My parents were not happy, but at least they tolerated me. I was not a bad person. Just without direction, they would say.

"My father spent many hours trying to get my attention to something I would like to do. But the more he tried, the more frustrating it became.

"My mother wanted me to paint the barn. It needed to be repaired and painted. Time had taken its toll on the barn over the years, and my father was busy with his clock making. Mother said I had to earn my keep, and I agreed to paint the barn to make her happy. I asked what color. She said, 'At this point, I don't care. Do something constructive. Fix the barn and paint it any way you want.'

"Well, that seemed not to have too many restrictions, so I inspected the barn and determined what needed to be done to prepare it for painting. I surprised myself and fixed the barn. Frankly, I was pretty proud of myself for doing so. So off to the village to get paint. I finally got to the village after wasting half a day just not doing much but did end up at the store. The owner of the general store proudly showed me his cuckoo clock that my father had made especially for him years earlier.

"I told him of my chore. He said, 'We have all these different colors. Pick one. They would all work.' I saw in the corner all the greens and reds and blues and yellows. My mind clicked, and I had an idea. I convinced the store owner to loan me his wagon, and I chose a can of each color and pulled the paint home in the wagon. I had a plan. I returned the wagon the next day and gathered up additional supplies.

"What was I to do? I decided to paint a mural on the barn. My mind was made up. I painted the village as best as I could at the bottom of a tall mountain. It took me all summer to do so. My mother just let me do what I wanted because she said, for the first time, I seemed directed into something I liked to do. I was focused and could not stop. I got up early and painted late into every day. And finally, it was done.

"My father and mother were amazed at the detail. It was beautiful, and I had found my talent. I had become a painter! And I dotted the countryside of the valley with murals for as long as I could. Families would contact me, and I made a great life doing so. I never married, however. That was a mistake. I was always to driven with my painting. But I learned. Next journey, I will marry.

"So my lesson to you and all is everyone has a talent. Even I had a talent. There is good in everyone, even me.

"Yes, I was a handful to my mother, but she gave me the space and patience to find my way. Those murals were my journey. I blessed the countryside with beauty and happiness. There were no moving parts, and my murals did not keep anyone warm like a quilt. But they did make humans happy and fulfilled in their own way. I had contributed like many others. I had found my way.

"Every human has a lesson and talent. Each just has to search until they find their journey and learn. That's what life is all about as a human. Find your journey and learn. Just be yourself, and your journey will come to you."

"Fritz, I am sure you are proud of your legacy."

"Well, I am. The murals are all gone now, but that is fine. They served their purpose."

Festival of the Catch

I open the portal today to the home view. The stumps are there today. Although the stumps are a bit uncomfortable, I like them, as it is purely natural all around me. No bench shipped in today.

So I have a seat on the stump and take a moment to soak in all that nature provides today. The sky is clear, and I am still amazed at the bright day with no sun. But hey, it's perfect in the Everywhere. No need for a sun here. The colors of the fall really bring out the beauty of nature. It's like a reminder of what nature provides just before a winter's nap.

Then in the spring, nature peeks through with the buds of spring. Like a teaser to remind you of our survival of the winter. Or the new growth of a new year. There I go talking to myself again. It must be an occupational hazard here in the Everywhere as I catch myself laughing again.

A spirit approaches and says, "Do you talk to yourself often?"

I say, "I talk to myself just like all other humans do. However, at least I admit it."

"Well, touché to you," she says. "My name is Lea. I was asked to join you today and tell you of my lessons learned."

"Well, thank you for being here. Who sent you?" I ask.

Lea smiles and says, "We just know. After all, we are all-knowing, all-powerful, and all-loving."

"Lea, what did you learn and bring back to the Everywhere with you this journey?"

"Well, I learned of balance as I returned. You see, these important items of life are blocked out during journeys. My journey would have been more easily understood had I known. Let me explain. I was born in the great north somewhere. I only know it was full of ice and snow most of the time and was always cold, cold, cold! My mother and father had prepared for me, as I had a fur blanket awaiting my arrival. We lived the winter around a fireplace in a cabin made of whatever my father could find, he told me as I grew up. The cabin was in a very small village of only a few dozen cabins, or shacks as some would call them.

"I grew up with little to see and learn. Most of my early days were spent just trying to keep warm. I only went outside when necessary. My mother would spend time telling me stories of her past. After all, other than stories, she had no other way of teaching me. I learned to cook and make furs into clothing as the skins were brought to us by my father. He was gone most days looking for food and firewood. He returned every day exhausted from his efforts. He said trying to keep himself warm outside was very tiring.

"But he never missed a day. He was a good father in a lot of ways. In the spring and fall, the only difference was the winds were missing. I could not see or hear the winds. The howling of the winter was gone and was a welcome change then. Only the summers were for activity, so to speak. I was allowed outside to play and exercise.

"It would always take a few weeks to get our energy levels up. Our bodies had to adjust to the outside. My father always said it was just old age trying to be shed for the summer.

"We only had a few short months of summer, so we had to make the best of it, including a lot of fishing and hunting, as my father spent his summers preparing for the winter. If not, well, I really don't think we could have survived. All the fathers worked as a team to make our winters warm and successful. All the mothers were out and about in the gardens, enjoying the fresh air and preparing vegetables for the winter.

"We always had to be on the outlook for bears, you know. They would come to the village at times looking for food. I thought they were just looking for friends, but I learned over time they were not friendly. I saw one of my friends dragged off into the forest once. A lesson learned for all of us.

"I think it was a reminder to respect the bears, as they belonged here too. It was a great lesson of Mother Nature. After all, as my mother would say, we are only here if Mother Nature allows. So we must honor nature and not abuse nature. We must use what nature brings us to survive. My mother was a staunch believer, as she told many stories of how Mother Nature ruled the lands.

"I had no schools to speak of. But my mother did have some books to teach me. She told me great travelers from the south would visit from time to time and trade with the villagers. Books were always a treat for us. Mother would trade skins and fats from the whales for books.

"Everyone loved blubber. My father and his friends worked hard every year to harvest whales for the winter. We always celebrated a catch with a festival of the catch. I always enjoyed those times. We also had to have a ceremony to thank nature for her bounties and gifts.

"Nature seemed to be what we worshipped and honored in the cold lands of the north. My father often said that's all we had to honor, and we must always listen to Mother Nature. She is there to teach us and provide us with safety and food.

"So I grew up with little to know and not much to learn, in a way. I always wondered what was beyond when those from the south would come and visit to trade. They told us all of great cities and wealth. And lots of toys. They also told us of schools to learn.

"I really wanted to go to school. But if I did, who would provide for me or where would I live? It was nice to dream about.

"As I grew older, I learned that I should find a mate—you know, get married. I had no idea what to do or where to go. My father said nature would provide the answers someday.

"I looked and looked and did not get any signs for a long time. One day, a group of hunters came from another village to help with the whales and to harvest for the winter. I met a nice young man. His name was Wok.

"Neither of us knew what happened, but I suspect nature had a way of making us meet. We knew almost from the first day we met we were to be mates for life. My parents noticed even before I did. A new festival was planned for Wok and me. We were married in the summer one year. Wok spent most of the summer building our cabin in the village. He decided to stay in our village, as it was next to the seas of the whales. So I did not have to move, although I would have gladly moved for Wok.

"We grew old together, having one boy and one girl. It's as if nature provided a replacement for each of us. Ours was a simple life. And that's all we knew. We had each other and our love, and respect for family, friends, and nature made everything worthwhile. Survival depended on respecting the values of each and every one. We surrounded ourselves with peace and family even when winter seemed unending and we questioned whether we would make it until spring.

"We lived by the laws of nature. There really was no choice. But in a way, we learned to enjoy our time on our journey. Wok and I had each other along with our children. We wrapped our lives around the stories we were told as children and taught our children the same.

"Yes, my life was simple and basic and fulfilling as a wife and mother.

"Wok and I uncloaked in the same winter. Our children had moved on to other villages by then. As we returned to the Everywhere, we were reminded of balance.

"We learned that humans had more to learn and provide us with more lessons. And I was soon to be reminded that my next lesson would be different than my last journey. I would find more to learn and see and even have schools. Balance will provide a journey to balance my last journey. I am excited to return. I do not know yet what or when, but I know it will be soon.

"I am packed and ready." She laughs. "I have all I need, you know. Just my values and me. That's all." She smiles. "After all, is anything else really needed?

"I will let you enjoy your journey now as you return. I am off to enjoy the colors of the fall. This is a treat for me. I have learned to love the Everywhere even more. Mother Nature is everywhere I look. It's so perfect here. I know that whatever happens on my next journey, Mother Nature is here waiting for me to enjoy.

"Best of days for you. May peace and love be with you.

"Just remember my lesson to you. Even on your worst, coldest, and loneliness of days, your values and Mother Nature are there to protect you.

"I am off to enjoy my day."

Spot

Good morning to us all.

I open the portal today to the home view. The bench is in its normal position, and the day is perfect. It's just a typical day in paradise, as humans would say.

Along comes a spirit, and I can tell he is in a great mood. It's very noticeable to me for some reason. I can always tell the mood of a spirit by its gate or the lightness of its movement. It's a giveaway. I laugh at my thoughts as he approaches.

He says, "Well, good morning, Billy. How are you this beautiful day?"

"Pretty good," I say.

He has a seat on the bench and says, "Wow, what a view we have today. Just look at all the fall colors."

"Can I ask a question?"

"Of course you can, but first, my name is Spot. What's your first question?"

"Since the colors of today are the fall colors, does the Everywhere have a winter view?"

Spot says, "Well, we could if we wanted to, but most spirits prefer the look of spring or fall. Summers and winters seem to drain the vibrant colors of nature. And that just isn't what spirits or nature wishes for our dimension. So unless someone has a specific request, it's a perfect day in the spring or fall for us all here. What's your second question? Hmmm?"

"Spot? Your name? It's a bit unusual, don't you think?"

He laughs and says, "Well, I was hoping you would ask. And yes, I knew you would." We both laugh.

"Well, I would like to think of myself as a human, but I guess I really was just a dog. But my family treated me like a human, you know."

"Did you have spots?"

"Actually no," he says. "That was the beauty of my name. I was a collie with a white neck and orange-brown fur over most of my body. I did have white feet for some reason, which always told my family of my whereabouts. I liked mud, and I couldn't play in mud without the telltale signs." He laughs.

"So why did you become a dog? Or is that stupid question?"

"Nothing is stupid in the Everywhere. Sometimes it's easier to learn about humans and how they are and the lessons they teach by being everywhere you wish to be and being seen without questions. My family allowed me out anytime I wanted to go free, so I was a neighborhood dog. I could go anywhere and join in, and humans could be who they were without being on guard. You know what I mean. It was great. I watched different families react to things that would happen and be totally different.

"If one of my friends, a boy, for example, threw a ball and it went through a window, one family was angry. They thought the boy did it on purpose. The boy's family said it was because someone bumped him when he threw the ball during pitch and catch. So they defended the boy. Didn't much matter. The window was still broken, and it needed to be fixed. But families would debate over who was at fault.

"Humans are a funny group, you know. Every action has a reaction for some reason. Humans say everyone is entitled to an opinion. Well, I guess that's true, but if you have ten humans and ask the same question, most of the time you get at least ten opinions. And most of the opinions are just pieces of the correct and incorrect answer. It was mind-bending for me to sit there and listen to the craziness of a human. Why is it that humans are treated so well by spirits? We learn a lot from humans, right.

"Well, I learned that the reason we do is every human reacts differently to everything. So how can you not learn from humans? It's an unending process just trying to keep up with humans. Sometimes, I would get so tired of listening to humans I would just go lie down and take a nap to ignore them. Besides, I liked naps."

"So what was your lesson?"

"Wow," Spot says. "I brought back many lessons. After all, being a neighborhood dog, I learned more than most humans every day. I observed humans who were just traveling through on vacation. They were very different than those who lived in the neighborhood. It's as if their tribes had different values and even different habits. Why are humans so different from each other? Must be that opinion thing again.

"Some humans are very polite. I heard the term southern hospitality. Not sure what that is, but the southerners always said please and thank you a lot. It was nice to see.

"And then I heard others speak of the brashness of New Yorkers. Whatever that was, who knows. What does *bada bing* mean anyway? Those New York humans were always in your face. They were always barking out orders like a dog. One New Yorker even tried to kick me once. And I was just trying to be friendly. He had the nerve. I could have bit him, you know. But like I was taught, I had to be a good dog."

"So why the name Spot? You never answered."

"My brother, a human, said I had no spots when I was born, and he thought it would be a good name for me. Everyone laughed, and voila, I was named Spot. It was that easy, and I was asked that same question my whole journey. Humans would ask, 'What's with your name, Spot?' I heard that so much I had dreams about in when I was napping. Sometimes, it was just hard to sleep because of it. My family would laugh at me sometimes when I napped because I twitched, as they would say. Well, if they didn't name me Spot, maybe I wouldn't have twitched so much."

"I have another question. I recently read where a body was discovered during an excavation in another country, and they found the remains of a being that appeared to be not of this world. It was protected and buried in a white powder for some reason. The remains were relatively intact. No one can determine what it was or where it came from. Could it have been some being from another world?"

"Before I answer, do you think the typical dog like me would have all the answers? I am flattered and will miss being a dog on my next journey.

"Well, let me explain. Aliens from another world? Well, first of all, the earth has been around forever, just like me and you. But humans have not been around forever. They came to earth not long ago. Spirits are always looking for new ways to learn, as you know. So this being you speak of. Apparently, it was from another time on earth. So was it an alien from another planet or just a being from that time on earth? Does it really matter? It was when you apparently weren't. Even a dog knows that." He laughs.

"Well, I guess you are right. Humans do not have ownership of earth."

Spot says, "But they just think they do. Hey, we dogs feel the same way. Humans live such a restricted life. They would learn more if they were neighborhood humans, you know. I was always learning from everyone, everywhere.

"A dog's life is great. I did bring back lessons from many families, cultures, and beliefs, not just my own. I spent my life listening and learning. Remember, dogs can hear many things that humans can't hear. I learned of many weaknesses of humans too. I remembered everything that humans would usually forget. And I could hear and smell things that humans could not.

"I was a super dog, and my family said so many times. And I was everyone's friend too. They would tell me everything. Even the children would tell me of their problems, even though they would not tell their human friends. I was a sounding board for many things. I could sit and listen to conversations in the park that no other humans could experience. I could sit in the hall in the school and learn from many classrooms at the same time.

"I could sit outside the church on Sundays and listen to those on the lawn just chatting and gossiping about their neighbors when no other human could. It was amazing to learn so much.

"But to most humans, I was just a dog. And to other dogs, well, they knew but would not share with humans either. We knew we could take back many lessons that humans could not experience. After all, that's why we were dogs. We learned so much.

"So dogs have a purpose in life too. I suppose cats do too, but I was never able to figure out what they did. They just irritated me and were always puzzling to me. Why were cats so popular? They are moody and always looking for a fight.

"But the real lesson for us all is about love. Most everyone loves dogs. For the most part, I was treated lovingly like family by nearly everyone. They were good to me. And if they were so good to me, why couldn't they be good with each other? That was one of the questions I could not answer but did bring back to share. Someday, we will find the answer to that question.

"Values lived and learned by humans are so varied, and yet they shouldn't be. Why is that? It's so easy to just follow the values. Dogs get it all the time. We love our family. We trust our family. We honor our family and always try to keep the peace, except for with cats. There is always a cat waiting to bother me. I just can't understand cats, but I guess all dogs have the same problem. I will learn more of cats, I suspect, on my next journey." He laughs. "You never know what happens next.

"Well I think I'll be going now. I have lots of spirits to meet and chat with today. Lots of love to share. After all, that's what dogs to." And he howls as he hovers away … because he can.

Learning from Nature

Good morning to us all.

I open the portal to the normal view. However, there is no bench or stump. This is a first. I see spirits all about but don't know what to do. I wait for several minutes, and it seems that I have been forgotten or the spirit is late.

I know this view well and begin to move slowly toward the brook and see if a spirit approaches. As I walk down the knoll, I realize just how big this valley is. The brook is further away than I thought. Distances are a bit skewed up here, as I am told distance and time do not exist here. Although I continue to walk to the brook, the brook does not appear to get closer.

Am I walking in place? What's the scoop here? I do sense I am making progress, though ever so slowly. I trust my instincts, as I know where I am and can see the knoll behind me.

After a while, I also realize how relaxing this walk is since it is so amazingly peaceful here. I can hear birds in the trees but can't see them. At least it sounds like birds. I continue walking and come up to a spirit. "Hello," I say. "How are you?"

"I am fine, Billy. And how are you?"

"I am not sure. I was to meet a spirit today, and I am not sure what has happened. The bench is missing, and the stumps are nowhere to be found."

The spirit says, "You are here as planned. Don't panic. I am sure she will find you."

"Who is to find me, may I ask?"

"Her name is Shea. She knows you are here. She will join you soon, I am sure." And the spirit moves on.

I continue my walk, and I can see the brook is nearing but slowly.

Another spirit approaches. "Are you Shea?"

"No, sorry. But Shea will be here soon. All is well." And he continues on. This is a bit dizzying to me. I have been walking for quite some time now, and still it seems the brook is quite a trek. This valley must be an illusion or something. It looks as if I have hardly moved from the knoll.

And yet I continue on.

Finally, after what seems like hours, I reach the brook. It is beautiful here with tall trees on the banks, allowing the brook to peek through to the sky and the knoll. I look back and see the knoll. It seems quite near, and yet I have been walking for a long time.

I see another spirit by the brook ahead, and I approach. "Are you Shea?" I ask.

She says, "Yes, I am, Billy. How are you?"

"I thought we were to meet by the knoll."

"Yes," she says, "I know, but I just got caught up here by the beauty of this view. The brook is so peaceful. I just could not leave when I came here by the brook. Here, sit next to me on that rock."

I have a seat and realize how tired I am. The brook, however, has a way of hypnotizing a person. I can't seem to take my eyes from the peacefulness trickling down the fall of the land. The water is so slow as it barely makes it over each rock only to fall a bit into a new eddy.

"I could sit here forever," I say. "This is really beautiful."

Shea says, "Now you can understand why I was late. I had a feeling about today. I did not decide on the bench or the stumps. I did not know why, but now I do. I was to meet you here by the brook, don't you think?"

"Yes," I say. "Do you have a lesson for me today?"

"Yes," Shea says. "I learned a lot on my last journey. I was born along a great ocean with mountains far in the distance. There were those who called it paradise. Lots of palm trees by the ocean. And beaches bigger than the biggest, from what I had been told. It was beautiful, with lots of humans living nearby. I had a family not far from the beach in a little hamlet woven into the forest. We lived close enough to the ocean I could hear waves in the distance. It was peaceful at night.

"My father was a carver. He would fell palm trees and carve boats for other families, and he built these arms made of branches of other trees to steady the boats so they would not roll over in the water. It was his invention, I think. He was always building these boats.

"My mother was not a builder, but she did love nature. Our home was tucked in the forest, and she made our area look like it blended right in. She was a master at this, as she spent most of her waking time outside in the garden or with me, teaching me of nature.

"I was an only child. My mother wanted more but said she just didn't have any more for some reason. So I was her prodigy, as she would say. I was to learn of nature like no other. I was to understand nature like no other. She taught me of trust with nature and to honor nature. She said many times our values start with nature, and peace will be provided to us by nature only if we live by the rules of the forest.

"The rules of nature were to follow your instincts. We come from nature, as she would say, so we should understand our roots as if we were like trees of nature. And the sun would feed our souls with kindness. She said the moon was only there to remind us of the sun while we rested for the next day."

As I listened, I realized her mother was her teacher too. Her father provided support, of course, but her mother was the master of learning.

Shea said, "I asked my mother once why the oceans never overflowed. After all, all the creeks and brooks and rivers all poured into the seas. Wouldn't the oceans eventually fill up and flood our lands? My mother said Mother Nature carried the waters back to the mountains to begin the journey back to the ocean. She said Mother Nature hid behind the clouds. I didn't quite understand that, but my mother was never wrong about nature.

"I understood water to be on a journey always. It was never-ending according to my mother. And we were to try to learn from the waters. We had to learn how to be never-ending too. She said humans were not here forever from the past, and she said if we could learn from nature, we could learn how to be forever in the future. Or at least try, she would say.

"My mother told me of great stories of the past and how storms, volcanoes, and winds swept away humans at times during great disasters. But the survivors always found the forests and the streams to still live on. Humans have to learn from this to be part of nature. She was convinced the secret of life was hiding in nature. We just had to find the secret. Studying nature was the way, and she taught me well.

"My parents grew old and tired from their efforts to survive over time. And they eventually uncloaked and returned to nature and the Everywhere. I did not learn of the Everywhere till much later. I spent my life in the forest trying to learn. And most every day, I would stop and watch the waters journey through nature drop by drop, only to return to the mountains again for another journey.

"I realized, after time, that humans do the same mostly. They begin their journeys as if in the mountains, only to eventually find the ocean, and then Mother Nature returns them to the Everywhere to return another time for a new adventure. Just like the water. But the only difference is water has been in nature from the beginning, and humans have not. So I still try to understand—what can humans do to make sure their future is the same as the water's journey? I still search for the answers even after returning to the Everywhere.

"I know I will return someday and want to bring my knowledge with me. I am told by other spirits that will not happen, as my next journey will be free of lessons to learn new lessons and return to the Everywhere all over again. Just like the water. But will humans be able to sustain life like the water? That is the big question. Water carries the values, I know. Do humans? Have they found the answer? I guess the only way humans will learn is to learn as a human.

"But the question I have is, will I return as a human, or as a tree, or as an animal, or as water? Who knows? Only Mother Nature knows for sure. And that's why I come to the brook, always looking for the answer. I know the answer is here along the bank of the brook. I hope to find the answer here someday. And if not, that is okay too. What better way to enjoy the day than to be surrounded by Mother Nature?

"I will keep looking though, and I hope you do too. Ask your fellow humans if they can find a way to live like the waters forever. And enjoy the cycle of life, as nature has since the beginning.

"It's a never-ending lesson of searching for me.

"I leave you today with that thought. Pass it on to others in your travels. Maybe someday a human can find the secret of the cycle of life too.

"Have a peaceful and wondrous day of life and nature. Love to you all." And off she goes along the banks of the brook.

Warrior of the Wind

Good morning to us all.

I open the portal today to a new view. I am on a steep cliff and not comfortable. The bench is here, and I have to be careful to make my way. It would not be that difficult if I was not afraid of heights. Others would freely make their way but not me. I have to brace every step I take because I am such a wimp when it comes to high places.

Finally, I take a breath as I have my seat on the bench. It's my safe spot here, as if the bench will protect me. But who am I fooling? A strong wind could cause me a problem at any moment. I am beginning to settle a bit as a spirit pops up over the cliff's edge, as if he took the elevator. He says, "Good morning! What a view!" He takes his seat next to me.

"I am Spoc." He looks at me and says, "No, not that Spock. He had pointed ears and was from a different planet. And he was only pretend anyway. I assure you, I am the real Spoc." He laughs. "Are you okay now? I know you are a bit queasy about heights."

I say, "I am a lot queasy about heights."

"Well, I promise you are safe here."

"Okay then, I trust you."

"Well, yeah," he says. "No need not to trust me. That's what we do here in the Everywhere."

"So what's with the view, Spoc? Why here and not down there in the beautiful valley below beside the stream or something?"

Spoc says, "I just love to come here. I love the view from above. I think I would be a great pilot, you know? Maybe someday on another journey."

Okay, I am settling a bit. It is beautiful here, I must say as I take a breath of what seems to be extra-fresh air.

"So, tell me why we are here today, Spoc. Give me a reason for this view!"

"Well, on my last journey, I was a warrior in a way. Although I never was in combat. My family needed my support when I was growing up, and the rulers needed men for their armies. So I joined the army to provide income for my family. I was also loyal to my home country, as my family was here long before the rulers. I came from a native tribe in an area just like this. As I grew up, my father taught me of nature's power and strength. I learned to climb mountains like this as a young warrior.

"We called ourselves warriors, but we never had to defend our camps or fight for our lands. We were just ready for anything, especially nature. So I spent my younger days high up in the mountains. Learning to thrive in thinner air made me stronger when in the valley. My father taught me that at an early age. He was a great teller of stories. Father taught me of my heritage and my tribe and how we survived the early days in nature.

"We learned to survive the cold of the winter by using skins to keep warm and to make our teepees. My tribe learned to travel with the seasons and followed the buffalo herd for food. They moved a lot, as they needed lots of grass and grains to survive. We learned to love and fear the buffalo at the same time. We honored the buffalo as our friend in nature.

"So yes, I was a strong warrior, and when the time came to help my tribe, I went away to join the armies. They had asked my tribe to help, and our chief agreed.

"We were scouts for the army. We would go out and find our way among nature so as not to be seen but to be heard. We had radios and could speak our language to other scouts who were able to tell our leaders of the movement of our enemies. Our codes could not be broken. Only our tribe new of the language.

"The other armies would look for us with their scouts. But that was not to be. We could travel among the trees and nature, and their armies would not know. They knew we were there but could never find us.

"We would enjoy their weakness and sometimes leave hints in their camps just to let them know we were around. We were ordered never to fight, for fear of capture, but only to be our army's eyes and ears.

"That was so easy for us. We did our part and defeated their armies. Our generals told us we were very important, and they honored us when we retired to return to the tribe. It was a great experience for all of us as we told our stories to our children and their children.

"I grew old being a great storyteller too. I had new stories to tell. Our tribe was successful, and we were able to live among the others now as we assimilated into the culture of the others. The army helped us understand them better. We maintained our own culture, and my family still does to this day. I listen and watch many days as I visit, especially during the winds. I can breeze in to see and enjoy my family. They can't see me, but they know I am there. For I can still go among the trees and not be seen. It's as if I was a spirit then as I am now.

"So we visit often, as our culture loves to know of our presence and our strength. We join in when they tell the stories of the past. It's so great to be with our families then. And yes, they can sense our presence. But they are not afraid. They are honored by our visits and know we are only there to watch and protect our families. After all, that's what we do. We are warriors of the world who are there to protect at any time needed.

"We are in the wind. And you will know if we make ourselves known to you."

"Spoc, did you marry?"

"I was honored by my tribe when I returned. Our chief introduced me to his daughter, and it was my honor to be her warrior. We had many children, and the first son eventually became the chief. Life carried on, and my son became a great teller of stories too. But then he could include the stories of the warriors of the wind. And that made me happy. He has passed the stories on to his children and their children too.

"My family, although all over the world now and mixed in with many cultures, has carried the strength of our tribe with them. They know of nature and of the lands and of the stories of the past. They carry our culture over time and tell all, sometimes through books, the stories of our past. It is wonderful to know how history teaches those of the future.

"It is sad to see, however, how some cultures do not learn of their past. They will miss many lessons. Ironically, because of this weakness, they will have to learn the lessons over again, and as humans say, history will repeat itself so they can learn.

"Humans cannot get along without learning. That's why we follow the humans so closely. They keep on missing history, and we learn again and again. And as humans would have it, they change history because of their mistakes too. They change the future and learn new things along with the old. If humans could just learn lessons and move forward. Wow, the earth could be so much better. It's as if humans are forgetful. But in reality, they are not. They just refuse to learn from history. That's why history repeats itself.

"Maybe the day will come when our stories of the warriors of the winds will be learned automatically by the generations. Wouldn't that be great? But till then, I make sure the stories get told. It is the honor of our tribe and our lands, so they must be told. After all, that's why I am here today. To make sure you know of the warriors of the winds.

"So now you know. And make sure you have a great a peaceful day. If not, I'll be there when you need me. Just call."

And off the ledge he goes in the wind.

The Secret to Success

I open the portal today facing a large body of water. It appears to be a great ocean. I can see far, as I am relatively elevated, looking down over a long, steady decline to the shore below. There is no beach to speak of, only large rocks and boulders shaped by the waves over time.

Time does not exist in the Everywhere, as I am told, but the rocks have been affected by a lot of shaping. "That's a good question to ask," I say to myself.

I do see spirits all about down below. Stumps are close by and seem to be here for today's meeting. The stumps, though part of nature, do not seem to fit here, as the trees all about are wind swept and lean in the same direction. Yet the stumps, though much shorter, appear to be different. Even the bark is different from the neighboring trees.

I have a seat and continue to watch the waves gracefully batter the rocks below. If I shut my eyes, I can hear the waves and imagine the power they bring to the shore.

I open my eyes, and next to me is my spirit all ready to visit. "Hello," he says. "Enjoying the view today?"

"I am and thank you. This is beautiful, and I can see and hear Mother Nature at work today."

He says, "Aye, you are correct. Mother Nature is proudly surrounding us today. She brings the waves to us to remind us of her power."

"Is there a moon close by that causes the waves like earth?"

He says, "No, not here. Mother Nature is a bit more obvious here. She does what she does when she wants to here. No need to blend in here. Mother Nature and balance are here front and center." He laughs.

"My name is Rory. I am pleased to be here today."

"Rory, I have a question. The rocks and boulders below have been worn from many waves over time. I can see the results, just like you. And yet I am told time does not exist here in the Everywhere. How can that be?"

"Aye," says Rory, "you are most inquisitive today. Well today is my treat. I wanted to visit my old stomping grounds. This was my idea. You see, today, you are here as my guest, and we are on earth on my old island visiting. We are, however, in our dimension, not to be confused with the dimension of humans. So what you see is mother earth's work here on earth minus any dimensional additions. Can you grasp that?"

I do understand. It's a bit easier now for me, having done this for a while.

He says, "In a way, this was what my island looked like before humans were here. Isn't it beautiful?"

"Yes, it is," I say.

"Some things just never change. The Everywhere does not change, as it has all views. It's just perfect here in the Everywhere."

"If I understand this, life goes on for humans here right now. They just can't see what we see."

"In a way, you are correct. They can see our view with their work from homes, roads, and other life they bring with them on their dimension. But I can walk among them in my dimension and enjoy my island any time I wish. It's just perfect. I don't have to bother humans, and they don't bother me. The spirits all around you enjoy this freedom too.

"However, as a spirit, I can walk through the veil of difference if I wish, just to be closer to humans to observe my family or my surroundings from when I was on my journey. I do on occasion. It's nice to visit from time to time."

"So, you are a ghost when you do that, right?"

Rory laughs. "No, I am not a ghost. Maybe humans think I am, but I am just me doing my thing, enjoying my day. I choose to be there in the moment only to observe and learn. All spirits can do the same as long as they came from their last journey.

"When I go on my next journey, the desire and reason to return here goes away. I will then focus on my next journey and enjoy the view then and after. Until my next journey.

"Yes, I know. It seems a bit complicated, but in reality, it makes it much easier for each spirit to navigate through the dimensions in an orderly way. Besides, there have been so many journeys, there is no way any spirit could keep up with all that has been learned since the beginning."

"So your time between journeys apparently lasts for centuries sometimes?"

"Hey, time does not exist in the Everywhere. I have been here forever just like you. And the last journey, whenever it was, was just a bit ago in the grand plan since the beginning.

"For humans, it may seem like centuries. For spirits," he says, laughing, "it's a blink and a wink. Let me make this clear. We don't forget our past journeys when we take the next journey. They become constant lessons for us all at that time. We just do not return to journeys past, just to keep life in order. If we didn't do that, it would be so chaotic nothing would get accomplished. We must continue to learn and not get caught up in the past. It would inhibit our need to learn.

"Balance provides this to us all to stay organized in our desire to keep learning. We just know what we know, and that is all-knowing, all-loving, and all-powerful. Knowledge is power, and to have such power, there is no need not to love all things everywhere. We are at peace with our journeys. And we honor our journeys by our knowledge, and we trust our journeys to be full of lessons.

"That is why the values are always with us. There is nothing more important than the values, Here, There, or Everywhere. And for those who ignore the values, great lessons lie ahead. Humans need to grasp this, and that is why you are here.

"As part of the wave, you are to teach humans to return and review the value of life and its purest existence. Values are to be followed to survive. After all, we provided you everything you needed as a human by giving you the values of life at birth. You, as a human, are to learn from this. Live and cherish these values as the secret of life and its existence. You are to have the values with you at all times.

"And if you don't follow the values, chances of survival as beings may not provide life in the future as humans. This has been explained to humans for centuries of time in your dimension.

"You are to reteach humans to return to the values for just that reason, to survive as humans. If not, you will simply self-destruct by war, famine, or the lack of ability to exist. You and the others are challenged by this as the cornerstone of your journeys.

"You may ask yourself, what happens if you fail your assignment on this journey? You will all return to the Everywhere, never to return here as a species on this planet. And if that occurs, here is what will happen. The earth human centuries later will have erased all that remained, and you will see what you see before you. A beautiful island here just like the rest of the earth. All will have been returned to its original view, just like you see. Mother Nature will have prepared earth for a new species so as to learn anew. Learning is a need for all spirits. We thrive on learning and being all-knowing. And nothing will stop our need to learn. If we can learn from humans, that's great. We have learned a lot so far. But if humans continue to lose the values they were given, the results will be what you see in front of you.

"And spirits will return here just like you and live a new life as a new being to continue learning. You will be given the values you need to live and learn as a new species, and life here will go on in this dimension.

"So I bring a great reminder to you of your assignment. Teach this to the other humans. It is your driven goal as a human to bring back the values to enjoy earth as we do in the spirit world. It's really quite simple. After all, how easy is it to live by the values? Ask yourself and others that same question and keep asking.

"It is, after all, the answer to life itself. The values are your connection to exist as humans on this wonderful earth.

"Enjoy your day. I have given you the secrets to success. Now go forth and do what you came to do on this journey. May peace and love be with you." And off to his island he goes.

The Cave

Good morning to us all.

I open the portal today to the side of a mountain. There is a small landing. This is an area that is relatively level and against the wall of the mountain, and there is a cave. It's as if, over the years, land was dug out in front of the cave, almost as an overview of the view of the valley far below. It's like an observation area. However, the cave seems to be natural. I am sure the spirit will tell me of the story of the cave.

I look around and can see spirits all about, pouring down the side of the mountain. As I am told, the spirits are returning from their journeys and checking in with their lessons. They will be glad to visit their family tree upon arrival.

It's like watching a bunch of children running down the mountain as fast as they can without falling so they can get home and tell their stories. Sure looks like fun.

When I turn around to face the cave, the bench is here, and a spirit is waiting for me. "Good morning!" he says. "I am Tug. Pleased to finally meet with you. I have been looking forward to my turn to visit with you, Billy."

"Tug, did you bring the bench? It was not here when I first arrived."

Tug says, "We spirits can do amazing things. I just made sure it was here when I arrived, and we will leave it at that."

I say, "I am not sure about waiting your turn. What does that mean? Is there a schedule?"

"No schedule," says Tug, "but we know of our plans, and I knew my turn would be soon. Hey, we spirits are all-knowing. So we just know. Have you heard that before?"

"Does this cave have meaning for you, Tug?"

"Yes, for me and many others too. The cave has been here forever. Many journeys took place here, as this cave served many. From the earlier times, you can see carvings, drawings, and etchings on the wall, as humans would leave their messages from their journeys. Archeologists visit here now to determine what era these came from. Should be fun since they came from many different times.

"This is like a cave hotel, as so many visited here at many different times. The cave offered safety from the elements during hard winters and protection from other humans and animals. Sometimes the inhabitants were hunters, and sometimes they were the hunted.

"There is a lot of human history recorded in this cave. And yet there were times on earth when this cave was unknown, only to be found and become a new journey and lesson. But the cave remained, and the stories of the cave lived on."

"And how about you, Tug? How did this cave find you on your journey?"

"I grew up in the valley below. As you can see, the valley is massive. Humans have often said you can see a hundred miles from here.

"I was just a human in the valley with my family. My father was a carpenter, so he came to the base of the mountain to get wood from the lumberyard. That was all he knew of the mountain, and he lived his whole life in the valley. My mother was a teacher of sorts. She would help those who needed help in understanding life in general. She would see and hear many things as she told those who needed help of great lessons from the past. She said she had a gift and could see things others could not. I did not understand her gift till later, but my mother was a saint to me. She was always there for me. She would heal my bruises and broken bones when I was young. Hey, I was a boy just being a boy. I was into everything and always getting hurt. That's what boys do." We both laugh.

"Me too," I say. "My Nana always called it mischief!"

"So life in the valley was wonderful growing up. My father would take me hunting, as that was the way for many of us to have fresh meat during those times. We were not wealthy like some, but we eked out a living, as my mother would say. But we were happy, though some were not. Even some of the wealthy seemed to be unhappy. I could never understand why, but it was true. My mother told me happiness comes from within. You only need your family, and love and happiness will always be around you. She said that over and over as I grew up. What a great mother I had.

"Well, times changed as my parents grew older. It seemed like the world was just passing by quickly when we heard of great unrest in lands not far away. There was war between our countries, and my father was really afraid and concerned. My mother tried to keep me settled, as I was still in my teens. As the war expanded, we saw signs nearby. Neighbors were joining the war. The enemies were ruthless and, from what we were told, killed for the sake of killing.

"Needless to say, my mother was to remain strong through all this. My father had no choice; he said he had to leave to fight for our country. I remember the day he left. My mother cried and cried. She was so sad. It was as if her heart was ripped from her. But my father settled me before leaving and asked me to take care and protect my mother while he was gone.

"He left, and I never saw him alive again. My mother changed that day he left. She became more quiet and careful in her ways. For some reason, she knew what others did not. She said it was her gift, giving her signals. I trusted my mother, of course. What she said was fine for me.

"One day, she sat down to have a talk with me. I thought I was in trouble. She said it was important that I grow up now and take responsibility for myself and our families around us. They needed for me to be strong. I was to prepare for the war, as it was coming our way. I should consider fighting in the war, but I could do so there and help more than leave to fight on the front.

"Over the next few days, I remember, we created a plan. I was to go to the mountain and observe and provide information. Once I got the information to her, she would make sure our neighbors knew so we could plan for the invasion. It was obvious from what she said that our country was losing the war. She knew before others. My neighbors trusted her, as they all knew of her gifts.

"So, I came to the mountains and found this cave immediately, as if I knew the way. My mother smiled when I told her what happened. So I was able to see far and wide from that mountain. I lived in that cave for several years as the war grew closer. I could see the front far in the distance. The fighting was intense. I would get information to my mother from notes I tied to my dog's collar. My dog was my best friend and a best friend to all my neighbors too. He was the fastest dog I ever saw. He knew exactly what to do, as if my mother had trained him like she trained me.

"I am not sure what my mother did with my messages, but she worked tirelessly each day and through the night. Our village worked behind the scenes to support the front lines and provide information, which led to the war changing directions and returning to where it came from. Over time, we were victorious, and my country was saved from the evil of others. I did my part, as did my mother.

"She grew tired, as the war had taken its toll on her. As I grew up and learned more. I learned that life has a way of teaching lessons. Those lessons my mother knew before they were lessons.

"My neighbors loved my mother, as did I. She was a hero to many as time passed. She eventually uncloaked and returned to the Everywhere. I learned later she had gifts like you. She had connections with the Everywhere like you, Billy. She could get information like no others.

"And then I knew why my mother's gift was so helpful.

"I became a carpenter like my father. It's as if I was to take his place in the neighborhood. Life father, like son, as they say. I was a good carpenter, as I had learned well. I never heard what happened to my father. I only knew that I missed him so much, just like my mother.

"But I was gifted by my mother. She had sent me a saint named Mia. I met Mia shortly after my mom's passing. She and I married and had a beautiful family. We had three daughters and one son, who was always into something. I believed it was mischief, as you say. Well, he was mischievous. And he broke many bones growing up. Like father, like son.

"My family was great and gave me many loving grandchildren over time.

"Mia taught them well. She would tell stories of my mother. Great stories as if she was here with her. Even though Mia said they never met, Mia knew of my mother and her greatness. Mia's parents told her of my mother. For that, Mia felt blessed and spent many nights telling my children of my mother. It was perfect in every way.

"I suspect my Mia had a gift too, but she did not share with the neighbors or me. She kept her gift to herself, I think out of respect for my mother. Mia knew too much not to be gifted.

"But then, who knows, now that I have learned so much since returning to the Everywhere. Many humans are blessed with knowing. And they are to teach others of the great lessons in life. Mia knew the answers. Love and family are where it all begins, she would say. And Mia lived the part, just like my mother.

"My children blessed me with so much love and respect over the years. It's all about passing on the lessons. And those stories echo through the cave behind us.

"I used the cave differently than others before me. Or did I? Just another story from the cave, I guess. This cave has seen many lives and lessons. And I am sure it will see many more.

"Make sure you have a wonderful and loving day. Peace be with you."

Pap's Reminder

Good morning to us all.

I open the portal today to the home view. The bench is in place, and all looks to be settled and perfect. I have a seat and see spirits all about. Although calm and perfect, today still feels special. And I can't seem to put my finger on the difference.

Then suddenly, I know! It's the spirit that just appeared next to me on the bench!

"Well hello, Billy! I have missed you!" It's my Pap. I am surrounded by so much emotion it's difficult for me to speak.

"It's so great to see you, Pap. Where have you been?"

He laughs as he usually does. "I have been around, not to worry. I know all that is going on with you, but then you already knew that."

I gather my wits, as this was unexpected. "Pap, this is all so overwhelming at times for me. What have you gotten me into?"

Pap says, "This was to be your assignment all along. After all, my journey was to continue our family on from generations past and create a solid foundation for you to learn. Your family has all done well to make sure you can move forward with your work for the wave. This has been planned since long before your journey. You are just part of the process to make this wave move forward. As you know, there is lots to do. You see it everywhere.

"Mother Nature is busy at work. There are happenings all over the earth. Balance has brought many spirits forward who have lessons from being not so good.

"Remember, for every valley, there is a mountain. There is an opposite for everything on earth. And yes, there is a good person for every not so good person."

"But it seems like there are more not so good persons today than before."

Pap says, "Well, it might seem like that because human communications are now more global than local. These things were going on before for as long as there have been humans. Tribes have always been in conflict. That's what humans do, so spirits can learn. But as the population grows, these lessons become a problem, much larger than the conflicts between tribes.

"Now these conflicts are camouflaging the real problem. As can be predicted even by humans, the population is growing to a tipping point. The earth is not large enough to sustain life for all humans. Something has to give.

"Spirits learn every day from humans. To be all-knowing, spirits have permitted humans to flourish and thrive as learning becomes more prevalent as we continue to learn more and more. Spirits need lesson upon lesson to maintain our all-knowing."

"What about other planets and other species? Don't spirits learn there too?"

Pap says, "Of course, but humans are special in a certain way. They are so unpredictable. The learning is always on, so to speak.

"It would be great to see humans expand and grow to other planets, but you know the rules. Humans cannot relocate unless pure of heart with the values intact. Mother Nature will not permit any expansion to other lands unless all habits are pure. Remember, you all come here with values, and that's it. That's how you return from your journey too. Only the values return to the Everywhere with you.

"Don't expect humans to relocate and expand any other way. Balance will not cooperate. Mother Nature will stop humans in their tracks. It will not happen. The Everywhere and all its dimensions are in place and have been successful all these years by being perfect in every way.

"To permit these habits of humans to expand goes beyond the natural process, and Mother Nature will protect the Everywhere.

"So the wave must be successful. You must do your part.

"Humans will have to learn like never before.

"They must return to their simplest understanding of life as it is to be known and lived. By the values. Period. End. No options.

"The population is growing, and survival is at stake now. Before, these habits of humans could be tolerated, as there was plenty of earth to support these journeys and for these lessons to be learned. But now that more journeys are needed here with the population naturally increasing, new pressures to exist come to light. The reality of survival as a species is not far into the future. A few centuries, maybe, is all that remains unless something is done.

"Earth will still be here as it always is. But humans? Maybe not. The values are less prevalent than ever before. And it is the wave that can bring humans to their senses.

"Yes, you and many like you are now in place, and many more will join you. But this is important work you do. You must not stop. I was here to prepare you for this. You have your family surrounding you to carry forward the message.

"Just think. What's more important to you than values?"

"Well, Pap, you know the answer to that. It's simple. Nothing is more important."

"During times of war or strife or famine or survival, all that is important for success is the values you brought with you. Everything else will fall into place if you just maintain and live by the values.

"Life has a way of always reminding each human, sooner or later. After all, that's all there really is. Humans just think there is more, and it's amazing to each spirit to observe and learn from this. Humans think they know everything, when really they know very little.

"What they don't know is none of what most humans think is important has any bearing on life. It's all hidden in the values they bring and nothing more.

"So how are you going to get that message to move forward?" Pap asks me.

"Well, Pap, I am moving forward day by day to make this known to humans, hopefully everywhere."

"Remember," Pap says, "you are not alone. There are many of you in the wave. It's important that you all join together in your own special way and help each other. This is a team sport, so to speak." He laughs. "You are all to support each other's efforts. So keep looking and telling your story. Keep reaching out to those that can pass this message forward.

"Think of it as a big barbecue. Keep it growing. Have more come to the barbecue each time, and eventually the lessons of values will spread far and wide. And then, and only then, will humans be able to expand and survive in other lands.

"This is not an option.

"Time does not exist in the Everywhere, but for humans, time does exist. And time is not on the side of humans.

"I must go now as I leave you to your work. It's been great to visit. But as you know, I am always here for you and our family.

"Keep the faith.

"Keep working hard.

"Keep moving forward and spread the message. The values will support you every day. They always do."

And Pap goes on toward the brook to meet with other spirits. After all, everyone knows Pap.

Taking the Fork in the Road

I open the portal to the home view. All is the same. Even the brook is in place. And along the brook, spirits are on both sides and in some cases in the middle of the brook. It sure is amazing to watch spirits move about without having to drag a cloak around.

The bench is here, and I have a seat to relax and watch life pass in front of me. I look to my right, and just along the bench is a spirit as if appearing out of nowhere. He laughs and has a seat and says, "My name is Gory. No, not the Gory you would think of but the last half of GreGory. I just wanted to be different."

"Gory, pleased to meet you. Before I learn of your lesson for me today, may I ask a question?"

Gory replies, "Well, of course. Fire away."

"Well, there are those humans who believe our lives are all planned out in detail and we are destined to follow that plan. I know we have assignments, as we have been told before. Can you expand on that?"

"Of course," he says. "In a way, your friends are correct, and in a way, they are not. Each spirit does have an assignment, but the topics or specific assignments are there because spirits want to learn in an orderly fashion so we do not miss the details. For example, you and Susie were to be married for this project. How and when you met Susie was not planned, but you were to marry. You just got married late in life.

"Your first son was planned so he could have Noah, who is and will be part of the wave. He will do many great things assigned to him. Your friend Bobby was there for you to remind you of love and family when you were away from yours in college. He taught you how friendship and love go beyond your immediate family. After all, you think of him all the time, and he was in your life almost fifty years ago.

"Your second son and stepson are to carry stories of the family and pass down to their friends and family. Stories of family and the chicken BBQ must be passed on for many to learn from. Your life has had certain assignments, and it was up to you to get there. After all, you are there on earth to learn, and if everything was planned to the detail, then there would be no learning.

"Spirits learn how humans react to different actions and reactions. It's amazing how different each human can be.

"We give you the basics and let you go. Each and every one of you makes your own decisions, but you must achieve the basic assignments.

"Does that answer your question?"

"So when Yogi says, 'When you come to the fork in the road, take it,' he is absolutely correct." I laugh.

Gory says, "Well, yes of course," and he joins in the laughter.

"Only spirits know if Yogi would have had the same experience had he taken either choice." And he pauses for me to think about that.

"Are you saying the choice may not be a choice but was predetermined?"

Gory laughs and says, "I am saying each choice is different but could be the same."

"Clear as mud," I say, and we continue laughing.

"On a serious note," I say, "tell me about your journey."

"Great! Be glad to. I was born to a very conservative family in a previous century. Even as a young boy, I was in church every Wednesday and Sunday, and we studied the Bible. It was a great learning tool for me.

"These stories of the past, handed down over the centuries, were awesome. Stories of great seas opening up to pass. And great floods of the world and predictions of the future. I was waist-deep, as humans would say, in my religion. This was the law of the land, as my parents would say. This is how we must live and worship. That is what I heard from the first time I could understand my parents. They were great parents, and I loved them so. They were always there for me, as a family should be.

"So I grew up in a small town, and my life was pretty predictable. My schedule was clearly spelled out for me, as my parents were filling my days with lessons and activities. The family participated by going to my games as an athlete and going to every school function, from plays to choir concerts. I was one of the few who tried to do everything. I was a good athlete but not a great athlete. I could sing and dance but was not the best, and although not the smartest student, I was above average. All in all, I was everyone's best friend, as they would say. Was I popular? I think so. I tried to make everyone my friend. At least I tried. Some of my classmates were not as accommodating, as they would try to bully me in my younger days. But I kept a stiff upper lip, as my father would say, and would bite my tongue and not fight back when I wanted to. I was to be a good boy growing up.

"But during that time, I had questions inside me that I did not want to face or ask. There were times I was troubled by what was around me. I was always thinking. And that can be dangerous."

"I know exactly would you mean," I say. "I have had my times too."

Gory goes on. "My parents wanted me to go to a Christian college and continue my path of learning. I was not so sure that is what I wanted to do, so I asked for their forgiveness, as I wanted to attend a large state university and fit in better. It was against their wishes, but they agreed, so off to the university I went. There were students everywhere. And courses of all career directions to consider. Do I become an engineer, a psychologist, a teacher, a doctor, or lawyer? Well, before I selected my direction in life, I was to take the typical college courses to expand my mind." Gory laughs. "All the time, students do this. They party hearty on the weekends around their studies and pretend they are sincere college students. At least that is what I learned in a short time.

"I was not happy, as I got caught up in the typical student life, but all along, I knew I was not doing what I wanted to do. I just did not know what it was. The fork in the road, as Yogi would say, was there for me every day. Do I study or not? That was the first fork each day.

"So, needless to say, I dropped out of college, only to return to my parents confused and upset at myself. My parents were understanding for a bit, and they gave me time because they knew I had to work this out myself. My girlfriend had gone to college with me, and she stayed. So, as expected, that did not work out. I found later that was for the best, as I was very different than she was; I just was too immature to know.

"So I finally agreed to return to college but to a Christian college with good principles and habits. It would be good for me. I began to study my religion seriously. And to do so, I had to learn of the other religions to verify my religion was the best choice for me and for humans. However, I found that each religion had its questions answered in a similar but different way. Each religion believed and taught its followers that their belief was the best and most truthful and honest for humans to follow.

"It was obvious to me that each religion was right and not so right in some ways. How could that be? At the same time, how could each religion be the right religion when each follower believed their belief was better than others? After all, that is why they followed one and not the other. But how could a Catholic, a Jew, a Protestant, and Muslim and on and on all be right? And the others not?

"I became even more confused.

"I graduated from Christian college with lots of questions and not so many answers. It was a hard time for me on my journey. I went to different churches when I graduated, and each belief tried their best. But I could not find the fit for me. Yet I needed to follow a belief. I felt compelled to do so.

"And then I came upon a church that seemed to understand. Religion was a very personal thing they would teach. But certain teachings hold true in each. Family, love, honor, trust, and peace prevailed in all. And the traditions of each were the real difference in each religion. It was the traditional followings of each individual religion that set it apart.

"So I began my own church. I called it the church of the sun for a while. It didn't quite hit my purpose. I tried other names like church of unity. Still did not attract members. I was saddened because I had, I thought, learned the secret of religion. I still looked and tried. And finally I started a church called church of the family. I did not care how many attended my church. I had determined that is where I fit in this world. I would keep my regular job as a teacher of subjects in schools. I would teach whatever the school wanted me to teach, and I did my best. But on Sundays, I would open my little church and just share my feelings and thoughts with those who were looking and could not find the answer for themselves. I taught the values, and to me, that's all that mattered. I helped some along the way. But any person from any religion could visit for a Sunday and learn my thoughts, and when they did, I knew it made sense to them. But they still returned to their traditions most of the time. I carved out a little following, so to speak. It was not large, but it was faithful to the values we all know come with us to earth and leave with us when we return.

"And to me, I did what I could. I was an early part of the wave, I am told. I got things started, I guess. I hope you can keep the wave moving forward. For me, as Pastor Gregory, I know my heart was in the right place. I know my goal was my values. It was easy for me to teach good common faith and understanding. Love and family can conquer everything. That's my story, and I am sticking with it. I grew old and not so tired and was happy with my life.

"My beliefs will carry on in time because I found the secret to religion. It is from within. The values are within each of us. All we have to do is share.

"I uncloaked an old man, happy with life and with all my questions answered. I went to the fork in the road and took it.

"Love and peace to you all."

McGee Gets His Stripes

Good morning to us all.

I open the portal to the home view. The bench is in position and waiting.

As I approach, I see a spirit perched and ready to visit.

"Good morning," he says. "How are you today?"

"I am pretty good, as usual." I have a seat.

"My name is McGee. Do you have any questions for me today?"

"Wow, McGee, you are ready to go today, aren't you?" I laugh. "Give me a minute to enjoy this view. You know, it never gets old."

"Okay," says McGee, "but I have been looking forward to my visit. I am glad you are enjoying your view today. Do you have any questions, or do you want to take a walk?"

"I love your eagerness to start our visit today, McGee. Okay, you first. Tell me of your journey as I continue enjoying the view."

"Okay," says McGee. "My pleasure. Well, I was born on earth."

"Okay, McGee. You can move along a bit faster. That I knew, or at least assumed I knew."

"My parents were mixed, as humans would say."

"Uh, McGee, what do you mean mixed?"

"My father was a cross between a collie and a German shepherd. And my mother was a mix of greyhound and coon dog."

"Oh. I say mixed-breed dogs. Okay, McGee. Now I understand."

"Yes," says McGee, "I was a dog. Is that a problem?"

"No, not at all. I just needed some clarification. All is fine. A dog, huh? Well I'll bet you have lots to tell me."

"Sure do," McGee says. "My mother was quite the looker. She was fleet of foot and could run with her long ears flapping in the wind. My father was the smooth, friendly, suave kind of dog." He laughs and says he was very confident with a cunning friendliness.

"So, when I was born, I had seven brothers and sisters—a big litter for any mother. Needless to say, she had her paws full. Get it?" And he laughs.

"I must say, McGee, you have quite the sense of humor."

"Well, I have been accused of that many times. After all, I had a bit of both of my parents and their parents, so I was a big, fast, loving dog with a great sense of smell. I could smell anything, and usually that was a good thing. But I did have my moments.

"So, growing up was full of energy for me. All I did was run and play. My mother loved that in me. We left her alone except when we were hungry. It did not take long, and I was almost full grown. Dogs grow much faster than humans, you know. Anyway, my brothers and sisters were being taken away. It was sad, and yet my mother told me to be happy for them. They were joining families who loved them from the beginning. You could just tell, she would say.

"But I was losing my playmates, and I was sad many times. And then there were only two of us left. 'Maggie and McGee,' she would say. 'What am I going to do with you two?' And she would laugh and slobber all over me. Must have been the coon dog in her. But that meant she loved me, so I tolerated her love.

"Then one day, a nice couple came, and Maggie was gone. I was so sad. We had become close, and it was so hard. My father walked with me to rid me of my sadness. He told me my parents would be by soon.

"And soon did not come for a while. I was stricken with the fear that no one would want me. I must say I was full of energy and always on the go. My father tried to settle me, but I was always full of pep.

"Then one day, a single man came to visit. He was in uniform. I could tell he was different than the others. I was not sure this would be a good fit. He took me to a playground of sorts and put me through an obstacle course. Before my turn, I saw other dogs have their troubles. Hmm. That was not for me.

"I went through that course so fast I think I even surprised myself. That was all that was needed. Officer Mark had made up his mind. I was to be his partner in the army. That sounded like fun!

"So off to the army we went. I had many obstacle courses after that. And I ran and ran. And after being in great shape and ready for the army, I graduated from boot camp, whatever that was, and I was now an officer. How about that?

"All I needed to know now was, what does an officer do? After all, I was a dog. So I went to training school. I was to learn many different smells at school. I learned about drugs and explosives and what to do if I sniffed them. I was my partner's partner, and I knew he would protect me from danger. And I knew I was to protect him too.

"So off we went together after finally getting to know each other well. We slept together at boot camp and school. I knew then we would sleep together when at war. All went well. I sniffed out one danger after another. Lots of explosives. My coon nose, as my mother would say, was a big help in my success as an officer.

"I did lose some friends, however. Their sniffers were not as good as mine. So they found danger too late sometimes. And as I was always told, there is no room for error.

"I had several medals by then. I had earned my stripes, as Mark would tell me. We were the best of friends. And we had tour after tour. That's what Mark called the trips to the war zone. Tours. I am not sure why they called them tours. It was no tour to me. I had to work hard every day just to stay alive sometimes.

"Since I had many medals, I was to lead other dogs into war. I helped train them with my nose. As Mark would always say, my nose knows. I trusted my nose. Can't get a cold as a dog, you know. Especially if you are in the army. Not a good thing." He laughs.

"Well, my students learned well. I taught them all I knew, and we became a good company of dogs. Our partners were really proud of our hard work.

"Then one day, I met my match. I was on guard running ahead of the trucks checking out the road, and I could smell a strong sense of danger. I stopped and tried to determine what and where it was. It was everywhere. I froze and signaled the trucks to stop. I carefully walked down the road, and the scent that I picked up was stronger and stronger, but I could not quite recognize where it was.

"I heard a buzzing of something. It grew louder as I slowly continued forward. I made sure the trucks had stopped. Mark called out for me to be careful. And then I realized it was a laser light that I had heard. And as I turned to run, this huge explosion occurred, throwing me a long distance into a big heap of a dog. I was stunned and dizzy. I slowly woke up with gunshots all around me. My soldiers were warned by the explosion, and they immediately began to fight back. The enemy was driven off. Yes, there were casualties, but only from the other side. My soldiers did well.

I must say that day changed my life permanently. I was in a stupor of sorts. I had trouble with my balance for quite some time. No bones broken. A few minor scars, and my ears rang for months. Eventually I was okay, I guess. But the army decided I was not to return to any more tours.

"Mark was to leave me and find a new partner. Now that was sad. Well they got me busy quickly then as I returned to camp to teach and tell other new recruit dogs of my experience. I was to show them the ropes or the smells and dangers of my lessons. I was now a master sergeant. A drill sergeant. Oh, it was fun. I loved barking orders to the new recruits.

"But they all learned my bark was bigger than my bite. I was a proud leader of my units, as I taught for years. And then one day, Mark returned to visit. He was bandaged up from injuries on tour. He needed to rest, he said. So he was going to retire and came to visit. It was great to see him. I slobbered all over him just like my mother did to me.

"And then he said, 'Want to come with me and retire?' 'You betcha,' I said. After all, he was my partner. We did everything together. So I was released from my duties at boot camp and school, and I retired with full honors. It was quite the sendoff, as I had amassed a bunch of medals over time. Even the big brass came to say goodbye. I was honored by their respect for me.

"So, Mark and I retired and went to his home. He had married since we were together. And he had two boys and his wife. I joined his family just like I had dreamed. And then he introduced me to Molly. Wow, she was the dog of my dreams. Needless to say, we wed immediately. I was not a dumb dog, you know. I recognized opportunity when I saw it.

"So there is where I lived out my life as McGee. I had many pups with Molly, and most went on to loving families. But there were two who made the cut and joined the army to keep the coon dog in them working hard. I was so proud of them.

"I uncloaked with my family around me. Molly was there till the end. Just old age I guess. My time was done. I returned to the Everywhere only to learn that this was my home from the beginning. Here, I smell peace and love and family every day. Honor and trust are all around. And there is not an enemy in sight or a smell I don't like."

I get up to leave, and McGee says goodbye. He wishes me well and hopes we can meet again soon. After all, that's what dogs do. They are everyone's friend, especially in the Everywhere.

Andy ... Tradition and Values

Good morning to us all.

I open the portal today to a beautiful view. It's not one I have seen before; it's different in a way. The bench is proudly perched under a tree overlooking a valley below. I have shade today, and yet I'm not sure why since there is no sun or star to provide the light. Yet I have shade. How cool is that.

I look out over the valley below and can see fields, as if someone cleared the land. There are woods sporadically strewn all about, as if the trees were added. Yet I suspect it was the opposite. At least on earth it's that way.

There are small ponds all about, but I do not see a brook or stream. Hmmm. Unusual. This view sure could use a stream to make it more perfect. I laugh at myself for being so picky.

Spirits are all about. Yes, there are mountain ranges in all directions. And they seem to be active with returning spirits. I am higher than normal, which makes the view even more spectacular. Wow.

I have a seat in the shade and begin to settle. I look to my right, and a spirit is next to me on the bench.

"How did you get there?" I ask.

She laughs. "Well, I can't say it's because I am fleet of foot. My name is Veranda. My friends call me Andy though. So you can call me Andy."

"I am honored," I say.

She is silent for a minute. And then Andy says, "Isn't this breathtaking? I just love it here."

"But this tree is magical. It provides shade, and I can't explain why."

Andy says, "I come here occasionally, and this tree is so special. All the spirits love the peace under the shade of this tree. It's like a personal protector for everyone under its limbs. No other tree provides shade. Hmm. Go figure."

"Do you think this tree might be Mother Nature hiding in the woods? Here to protect all who stand under her arms of peace?"

"Don't know," says Andy, "but I love the idea."

"So, Andy, what brings you here today instead of another spirit?"

"Pap asked me to stop by and say hello and visit. After all, we are from the same family tree. So everyone says hello."

I am silent for a minute. I have this overwhelming feeling upon me like goose bumps on my arms. "Andy, you caught me by surprise. I am humbled by your visit today. Almost teary-eyed to see a family member here with me. I miss my Pap and everything about him."

Andy says, "We all know how you feel. Pap and all send their love, of course. You are special in our hearts. After all, you have a big assignment to achieve. And we all know the importance and values you must teach. We know and trust you will provide the message to many humans. But not to worry. You are not alone. There are many around you supporting your efforts as you support theirs."

"Thanks, Andy. I needed that. Not a day goes by that I don't work on my assignment. That's for sure. So tell me, Andy, of your last journey."

"Well, I'll just do that," says Andy. "I was born in a barn." she laughs. "Hey, that's better than a field. My family were the best workers around. My father was famous for his strength and endurance. He could go all day. My mother was a bit dainty, but she managed to pull her own, as humans would say.

"I grew up frolicking in the barn yard, and in time, I was allowed to run in the fields and get plenty of exercise. Life when I was young was so much fun. I loved the freedom to run and run. Yes, I could run with the boys, as humans would say.

"Being a horse has its advantages. And I was big and fast. So many a human wanted to own me. But I was not for sale, ever.

"My human family loved me. They shared all their secrets with me. I overheard many conversations that other humans never heard. I knew everyone's likes and dislikes. No one was afraid of me. I was like a gentle giant. And my human family took great care in making sure I was always safe and protected from others.

"And in the spring, I was out there in the fields with everyone. I was the lead horse for many a chore. I always said it was because of my good looks and brains, but in reality, I was the best and strongest of them all. I taught many brothers and sisters how to do their jobs in the fields. It was an honor to be so important to our farms."

"Farms?" I ask.

"Oh yes, my human family grew over the years. They acquired more farms in the area, and I traveled with the harvest team to all the farms. The families would shock corn and tie off wheat and oats most of the summer and fall. I pulled wagons of grains and sometimes families from one farm to another. Everyone loved me. I felt so special.

"On occasion, my family would have plowing contests just for fun. I loved these pulls. I would get so excited it was hard to hold me back. Pap would take the time to calm me. He was so special with all of us. He was very young then and had a way with all of us animals. He had this gleam in his eye during the pulls. He would lead me, teamed up with Buck, my partner. He would lead us to the pull calmly and quietly. We would back up to hook up to the plow.

"And when Buck and I would look at each other and nod we were ready. Pap would say, 'Giddy up,' and off we would go. No team could keep up with us. We were awesome, and Pap would be laughing all the way. He had so much fun with us. Gosh that was fun. Those where the good old days.

"My life as Andy was wonderful. I went everywhere with the family. I never wanted for hay or oats. My entire family was treasured by the farmers. I had a colt or mare almost every year.

"I lived a long life for a horse. I knew of the history of our human family, as I heard many stories being told, especially during the harvests. When all the families were together, great stories were told during rest time and meals. It was like a tradition each year for all to see. They came from miles around to say thanks and to help with the chores in the fields.

"Your Pap was quite the human. He helped everyone in need. I was there to see it every time. Your family, long before your time, had a tradition of being there for anyone who needed a hand. Nothing had to be said. Your Pap knew what to do and when to do it. That tradition lives on today, as you know. Pap learned that from his Pap, and his Pap learned from his Pap. What a tradition over the years.

"It was my honor to be part of the family. I loved you all and all your family stood for. Their values live on today in you and others in your family. Family, honor, trust, love, and peace. How perfect and easy it is to live by the values. Life is so easy when the values are all you need. There is no want for power or greed. No need for influence from others. No need for anything but each other, for when you have each other, that's all that is important. Pap told me so many times in the barn. I taught my family as well."

"So how did you get your nickname?"

Andy laughs and says, "That was your Pap's doing. He did name me Veranda when I was born. And everyone thought it was a cute name. But as I quickly grew, he would watch me run in the fields. One day, he said, 'You are more than just a Veranda. You are really special. And you need a special name. I am going to call you Andy. You can work with the best, so you should have a special, loving name. I am going to call you Andy from now on.'

"I will never forget that moment when he donned me Andy. I could see the love in his eyes, as he treated all of us with so much respect and love.

"Our family tree is wrapped with that same feeling, as you know. So as you continue on with your work, remember to work hard, harder than everyone else. After all, that's what your family does. And keep the values around you and teach those who cross your path the power of the values. That's the easiest and hardest assignment there is.

"I pulled my weight in my day. Now it's your turn. Pass this on to your family and those around you. Make everyone part of your family, as Pap did in his day.

"So now you know the secret of how our family tree is so large. We are everywhere in the Everywhere. And Pap watches over us all.

"May you have a peaceful and wonderful day today. Love to all …"

The Neighbor's Farm

I open the portal today to a different view. I am on a mini-island in the middle of a lake. It's maybe an acre or two with a small grove of trees. Grass and flowers are all around me with the bench. The lake is surrounded by mountains, which are high and steep, and they angle right to the edge of the lake on both sides and behind me. However, there appears to be a bit of an opening ahead of me, as if it is an area for the lake to find its way through the mountains.

It's like I am in a huge bowl. I can almost sense an echo as the wind flows through the trees above me.

I can see spirits on the shoreline all about me, as if they have come to the water's edge to observe the beauty. There are a few roaming around above the water, taking a shortcut to cross. "Must be nice to be able to do that," I say to myself and laugh. Someday I too will return here to do just that. Wow, that is the first time I have acknowledged my return.

I snap out of my daydreaming as I notice a spirit directed toward the island. And then, well, he is here. Funny how that happens so quickly.

"Hello." he says as he has a seat next to me. "That was fun. I always love doing that. My name is Yon. How do you like this view?"

"Pleased to meet you, Yon. This view is awesome. And the lake is so majestic. I can understand how the wind is above me in the trees and yet the lake shows no sign of movement since it looks like a mirror. See how the mountains glimmer on the top of the water? It's amazing."

He laughs and says, "Now you know why I love it here. It also reminds me of my last journey."

"Where was your journey?"

"It was in the lands called Scandinavia where the fjords are even more extreme. But this is almost the same. See how the mountains are almost like cliffs? Well, I used to live on top of the mountain like this and could look down to the ocean below where it sliced its way deep into the land. And many villages were on the water's edge at the bottom of the mountains.

"My family were farmers in a way. We had short seasons, so we were extremely busy for only a few months in the summers. Winters were long and cold, but we had plenty to do then too."

"Did you have a large farm, Yon?"

"Well, yes, in a way. We had lots of land, but only some was flat enough for farming vegetables and grains. We had a few cows for milk and owned two horses, as reindeer were easier for us to take care of. Reindeer loved the cold and snowy mountainside and needed little shelter. The horses and cows needed a barn to keep them safe in the winter.

"Our springs and summers were full of activity in the fields. And our autumn was a scramble to gather firewood for the winter. It was our custom to plant two trees for every one we felled for our survival. My family always did that for as long as I could remember. So our woods were pristine and beautiful, unlike other areas.

"My father was a rugged old man by the time I was born. You could tell that he had survived many winters. His face was full of wrinkles where the summer sun had taken its toll. The sun is difficult, as in the spring it ricochets off the snow and into our faces. We burn easily, having been inside most of the winter. My father said his face was the result of many wars with the sun, and he always lost.

"My mother was a seamstress, as all mothers seemed to be in the land of the north. Everyone made quilts, blankets, and clothing. My mother learned how to sew leather since we used leather for our coats and gloves. She was a master leather craftsman. My father was quite a wood carver, as he spent his winters by the fire staying warm and carving. He had so many old tools he had passed down to him from previous generations. He spoke of my grandparents often since I did not have the chance to meet them. They had uncloaked before I was born.

"I heard many stories of bravery during the hard winters. It was fun sitting by the fireside and listening to all the lessons of life.

"I had one brother and one sister at home. My other brothers, three of them, had already moved away by the time I was born. Two became sailors in the navy, and one was a fisherman by trade. He lived in the village by the ocean and would visit often.

"I only met my oldest two brothers once when I was little. They had been in the navy during the war, and their ship sank from a sub attack by the Nazis. My mother was so distraught for an entire winter. My father was shaken to his core as he sat in silence for days on end.

"I was sad, but it did not hurt as much for me since I was so young and had only met them once. It always bothered me though as to why I was not as sad as my parents. I always felt guilty in a way because of that.

"So when my other brother would come home to visit, it was extra special since he was the only older brother left in the family. He was my favorite brother. He and I seemed to have a special bond.

"My other brother lived at home, and we fought like many brothers do. We were not as close. He said I was spoiled and got everything I wished for because I was the youngest. I could never understand that since I mostly got his hand-me-downs. Most of my clothing were his at one time. Makes no sense to me. But that was my big brother. He was impossible sometimes, but you know, he was my brother just the same.

"My sister, well, she was with my mother constantly at her side, learning and listening to the ways of the north and how to survive as a woman. My mother was always teaching her something.

"And for me, well, I was much younger, so I was the listener and the learner. I was always following someone. Sometimes my father would drop me off at the neighbor's just to learn from him. He was a crusty old soul. He lived alone, as his wife had uncloaked before I was born, and his children had moved away. I think my father wanted me to help him since he was so old and had difficulty getting around.

"He liked me a lot, and even though he was gruff and mean at first, we became friends. I became his sidekick. You know, he was like my grandfather maybe, since I did not have one. So in a way, I adopted him over time as mine.

"I think my father enjoyed watching us become friends. My father was always busy doing something. He was a good man, hardworking and all, but he kept his distance. I think losing his older sons hurt him a lot.

"He got even quieter as he aged. The burden of the farm was taking its toll, I suspect. My older brother was helping him almost daily then, and I was helping my adopted grandfather. So my brother and I began to become friends as I grew older. I believe he respected me for working so hard to help the old man.

"As time passed, we had learned a lot from both my father and our neighbor. We knew how to survive at least. But did we know how to live? Neither of us knew what living really meant. All we did was learn to survive. There was no other choice. There was no time to live and do other things. After all, we did not know what else there was to do with our life. We could only dream.

"My brother said once to me, 'Maybe the dream is better than the reality of what life really is like to live. Maybe our parents were just protecting us from everything else.'

"So one day, without me around, my brother asked my father about life off the farm. What was it like? Was it worth dreaming about?

"Our father said, as my brother told me, 'It is where your brothers were taken. It was their wish to find what it was like to live off the farm, and they learned it was not as much of a dream as they had wished. And life took them away before their time.' Father would say this many times.

"All we knew is what we knew. We knew how to survive, and we lived using the values we knew of. Family and love for each other was important. I even learned to love my brother.

"Trust? We had to trust each other, or we couldn't survive the winters.

"Honor? Well, there is no other way to live in the north. Honor was a must.

"Peace? For us, we only knew peace and learned what lack of peace meant since my older brothers were taken when peace did not exist for them.

"So that's all I knew.

"My brother was more driven than me. My father agreed for him to leave one summer. He said, 'Go and find your way. And if you find what you are looking for, so be it. But if not, you return and take the farm. I will be waiting for your decision.'

"So my brother obliged and left. So here I was helping my father and my adopted grandfather in the summer. That was a long summer. Up early and in bed late. Every day with so much to do.

"My brother came back that fall with a wife in tow. He said it was love at first sight. It must have been since the summers were so short. I teased him, but it was good to see him again. And besides, I needed him back. It was too much for me that summer when I was alone.

"So he took over the farm, and my father began to slow down and age gracefully, he would say. My adopted grandfather did not fare as gracefully in his old age. He suffered that first winter, and I almost lost him a few times. But he managed one more summer with me at his side. And then the day came when he just could not go on. I was at his side that day.

"He told me he loved me like a son. Well, I have to tell you that hit me hard. As I had realized all those years with him, I had loved him like he was my grandfather, and in a way, I guess he was.

"As he passed, he told me the constable would be by in a few days to talk with me. And he returned to the Everywhere as I stood there. I sensed he left his human body. I could almost see it happen. And then all that was remaining was his cloak. He had asked me to put his body out behind the barn in a grave. That is where he wanted his cloak to be. So with my family there, we did just that. We wished him well on his new journey. We did not know exactly what that meant then, but he had told me he was looking forward to his next journey.

"Two days later, the constable came by and gave me the papers to his farm. He had left the farm to me instead of his sons who had moved away years earlier. According to his letter, they had no interest in the land. They had found another life off the farm.

"So there I was a land owner like my brother. You know, I had to make a decision that day. Was I to follow my other brother who was a fisherman and do something other than farm here, or do I stay here and do what I know what to do?

"My brother and I talked for a long time that day. He agreed to give me a summer to learn, and he would run both farms for the summer. So I went to the village by the sea that summer. Well, I was like a fish out of water, as humans would say. It was not for me. I knew what I wanted to do. So I was planning to return to the farm, and well, there she was, love at first sight. I laughed at myself that day. Not long after that, my new wife, Gerta, and I returned to the farm. I was my brother's neighbor now. We became the best of friends. My parents uncloaked later that year. And my brother and I had great lives farming next to each other. We had learned all we needed to learn. And we too gave our children the opportunity to choose. We taught them as much as we could and let them make the best choices for themselves. We were happy to know they had choices.

"So my life was spent on the farm, and I had a great life. My youngest son decided to stay and take over my farm. Déjà vu all over again, I guess.

"Life was full, and my time to go the next step came quickly that one summer. My next journey is right here. Not a journey as I thought but a return home. And now the dreams are all answered. This was my home all along. Back in the Everywhere where we all belong.

"May peace and love be with you.

"Enjoy your journey as I did."

Understanding the Wave

Good morning to us all.

I open the portal today to the home view again. How invigorating it is to be here. This is so perfect here. Even the bench is perfect. I have a seat and enjoy the moment. As I look about, all things are the same. Even the spirits, whoever they may be today, are peacefully enjoying this view and visiting with others or enjoying a peaceful moment alone. It appears everyone understands and respects each other. It's like an orchestra of love and peace. The flow of the spirits all about should have music in the background. I laugh at the thought, but that's just how wonderful it is here.

And as I finish my laugh, I realize there is a spirit next to me. I look over, and she begins to laugh too. She says, "Gotcha," and continues laughing.

Nothing else has to be said. We both continue to observe the view in peace and calmness. It's as if we are watching a movie, and everyone knows their place and lines. There is a flow of happiness all about.

Then I say, "I know you probably don't understand, but this is like a Hallmark movie." I laugh.

She joins in and says, "But you forget, Billy. We are all-knowing. And you are correct; it's just like a Hallmark movie.

"My name is Eva, for Evalyn. My mother blessed me with Eva. 'I always loved that name,' she says. I can't explain it, but the name Eva is so warm and friendly. I could feel that on my journey almost every time I met someone new. So thank you to my mother."

She laughs. "My father had other names he wanted for me. But as my mother said, 'When you were born, even he knew your name was to be Evalyn, or Eva.'"

"Well then, I feel I can ask you a question. I sense you have the answer."

Eva laughs and says, "Hey, that's why I am here today."

"Okay, I know of the wave—many have told me of the wave—but no one has exactly explained the wave."

Eva says, "Well, let me see if I can best explain it. As you know, our journeys are full of assignments. We are to learn on every journey. And humans, well, they are very good examples to learn. Humans are very unpredictable, so we are always learning."

"Yes, it's true, they are unpredictable."

She laughs. "So remember, each of us, you included, began your journey with nothing more than yourself and the values you brought with you. Family, love, honor, trust, and peace—that's it. And all of us in the Everywhere fully understand that's all we need on our journeys. And when humanism takes on our journeys, power and greed and fear especially cloud over our basic values.

"Remember, time only exists on journeys. So over time, as history has shown, power overwhelms, greed takes over, and humans are mistreated. Sometimes religions are to blame. After all, many wars come out of those who believe their religion is the way for all to learn and follow. Disagreements or debates turn into wars and, in some cases, last for years and even centuries. Such a waste of time, but that's what humans do. They forget about their values and permit those with power and greed to wield fear on others by war or control in many different ways.

"No human deserves that. No humans should live in fear or be controlled by power and greed. And yet humans are such beings that someone or a group must lead others to be civilized, as humans would say.

"And this is where waves occur. Remember, we all arrive with assignments. Our goal if we are part of a wave is to overcome the power, greed, and fear and return to the values we brought with us.

"Over history, you can study how waves or even wars occurred, and humans learned and overcame power and greed. Those were waves of spirits who came to return humans to the values.

"Humans have prospered, as you know. However, power and greed have maintained a grip on many humans. Those that lead are to lead with values in mind. And yet power and greed have overtaken this gift of leading in many ways.

"And now earth is fast approaching a point where humans will need to find new ways to survive or they will self-destruct in some way. They will either starve from overcrowding, or war with each other, or elimination of many who just follow the values. None of those choices bode well for humans.

"The only other option is to relocate and expand to another planet. We in the Everywhere have a specific understanding. To maintain perfection in the Everywhere, only those who can relocate can do so with values and nothing else. There can be no power or greed.

"There are those who want to expand to other planets with power and greed in mind. I can tell you now that will not happen. It is literally impossible for a human to survive with anything other than values.

"Hence the current wave. Yes, we have had waves in the past, as we discussed. But this wave is the most important, as it may very well be the last wave to correct the human ways. There is too much power and greed in today's earth. Fear is everywhere. Not the fear of falling or the fear of drowning, for example. But fear of being controlled by others.

"Power and greed must be eliminated for humans to survive. Those in control must not gain over other humans but lead by using their values. I should know, because I was part of this wave. I was one of the first here. And now you are part of the wave.

"In our own way, on our own journey, we each have, along with many more humans, an assignment to return the values to the forefront. In some ways, it is to return to our past. Not return to ways before electricity, for example. But to return to ways humans live and prosper from their hearts, so to speak. Family, love, honor, trust, and peace. The purpose of this wave is to return to these values.

"Think about it. Is that such a hard task? No, not really, but sad to say, it is because of power and greed. Governments in your time are perfect examples. They are to lead with the values, and yet they lead for their own benefit of power and greed. It's evident just about everywhere, and frankly, the wave must overwhelm this and return to the values.

"After all, there are no other long-term options that will work. So the wave is here and in full force. Whether it's you writing a book to teach others or the Hallmark movies, or in my case, I was a nun and teacher in an elementary school, we are to do our part and inspire all humans to return to the values they came with. It's the natural thing to do.

"In my case, I was a nun, as I said. I was to teach my religion to my students, but in reality, I was to lead by using and living by the values as an example of a good life to live. I was loyal to my family and loyal to my beliefs, but I was loyal to the values more than all others. I knew of other religions and beliefs, but they all possess the values.

"It's true, each religion has its way, but none are the complete answer. And yet humans follow usually only one in their lives. But beyond and above all the earthen beliefs, the values exist or should exist in every ideology or government.

"That's the assignment we all have. Make this happen for the good of all humans. We in the wave must make humans see the forest in the trees. Every human has values; we just have to make each human use the values once again. That, my friend, is today's wave."

"Wow, thanks. I needed that, as we all do. I do my part every day. I do not waver. It's sad it took me so long to get here though. But now I can see my assignment clearly. Tell me about our part of the wave. How did you become a nun?"

"Well, my family was wonderful. I was blessed to have parents so loving and trusting. After all, my name alone was a big help. I was part of the wave the day I was born. Just didn't know it at the time, of course. I had three sisters and two brothers. You know, good Catholic families are usually large." She laughs.

"My sisters were wonderful to me. I was the youngest, and each one spent much time with me, teaching me and loving me as their sister. My two brothers, well, I think they were in my family as a test of our existence." She laughs. "They were always getting into trouble when they were growing up. They roughhoused and got into fights and such. My mother accused them of being heathens.

"My father was strict in a loving sort of way. We girls had to be pure and loyal to our family and our rules. Father made sure of that. I know he loved us very much because he was always protecting us. He did have to teach my brothers many times, however. He used the walk-to-the-woods method of teaching many times, and it was difficult for my brothers to sit after those walks. But my father would always say, 'I love you, and this will be good for your soul,' and off to the woods they would go. We all knew our brothers would return with lessons learned.

"You know, they both grew up to be good brothers. My one brother became the head librarian at our local university. He taught for years and aspired to be in the library. He achieved his goal and set up many programs to lead many to learn about life and values in his own way. I was always so proud of him. My other brother, ironically, became a policeman. I doubt he ever took anyone for a walk to the woods, but I know he was best friends with all my children in my classes. He was a good man and loved oh so many humans. He did right by our family, as my father would say. My parents were very proud parents.

"My sisters, one by one, fell in love and married their best friend, it seemed. They all became very successful mothers and leaders in our community. They taught the values in their own way. First through their children and then through their neighbors. They were always helping others in any way they could.

"I was different, however. I loved everyone but had no desire to marry. I am not sure why. I just wanted to help and teach and love all. So one day, it came to me to be a nun. I sat with my parents and told them of my plans. I must say, my mother cried with happiness and was honored by my decision. She knew my life would be very different than the others' but, in a way, very similar. She knew, without knowing for sure, I was part of the wave.

"For I was to teach many children in my life. I hope I helped them all follow their hearts and their beliefs, but I knew the values were at the core of life and happiness. Love was all there was to me. I loved everyone. I lived my life to the fullest. I helped as many as I could. I really don't think I ever met a bad human. Some had power and were greedy, yes, but I think I was able to reach them sometimes. And I helped them mend their ways.

"When I uncloaked, it was a happy day for me. I was calm and ready for the moment. I had achieved my assignment. I followed the values and taught the values. I think everyone should be a nun." She laughs.

"Returning to the Everywhere was so natural for me. For I knew. After all, I was part of the wave and knew it. Over the years, I learned the ideology of Catholicism was just fine, but even above the belief, the values were the core of life itself. So returning to the Everywhere was perfect for me. I was ready whenever my journey was over.

"So you must do the same in your own kind of way. You have many lessons to teach. It may not be as easy for you, but it is every bit as important. Each of you in the wave must not waver and keep your focus. You will do well by touching everyone's heart with your way of the wave.

"I wish you only the best. May peace and love be with you always. I know you will succeed. Keep smiling, as you always say." And then Eva is off to enjoy her day.

The Quality of Goodness

Good morning to us all.

I open the portal today to a new view. It looks like earth, but I sense it is not. It's a beautiful view with a small creek and two stumps that are overlooking a large valley with a mountain range to my right, high with snowcaps. To my left, the creek continues on and winds through a great valley that goes on to disappear into the horizon. There is a moon too, which looks much larger than ours on earth. The plants and trees are green, but the soil appears to be more blackish than most soil on earth. Only a farmer, at heart, would notice. I read recently where a similar planet to earth was located about 111 light-years away. Using conventional space travel as we know, that would not be feasible to relocate humans. It would take hundreds of years or more to arrive there. Wow. It's overwhelming to realize the massiveness of the Everywhere.

And yet I may be there now, or on some other similar planet, or in a dimension not yet discovered or noticed. But I have my seat, just the same, still in awe of what my blessing brings every day.

And yet, wherever I may be today, there are spirits everywhere enjoying the moment, the day, and whatever life brings them. I can tell the purity of this planet, as I am high enough overlooking the creek to realize the water is so clear I can see the creek bed below.

Suddenly, without much fanfare, a spirit approaches, saying hello as he nears the stump. I reply with, "And good morning to you. What a beautiful planet today."

"Ah yes," he says. "I thought you would like this planet. This dimension is just as you would expect. Pure and beautiful. My name is Mutt. Actually, my mother named me Ronald, but not long after I was born, I gathered the nickname Mutt. And it never left me. My friends all called me Mutt too.

I was always identified as Mutt. In fact, on my uncloaking, my headstone name was Mutt." He laughs.

"How did you get that name?"

"Well, one day when I was young, my parents brought home a dog. My dog was immediately drawn to me. I think we were destined to be good buddies all my life, or at least most of my life. He was so friendly. I loved him. As we were playing with our new dog, I asked what kind of dog our new Jackie was, and she said he was a Mutt. I asked what a Mutt dog is. She said, 'Well, in a way, Jackie is like you,' and she laughed. 'You come from a long line of humans with different backgrounds. Your ancestors are from all over the earth, so in a way, you are a Mutt.' I understood enough to explain to my friends that Jackie and I were both Mutts.

"And from then on, my new name was Mutt. And frankly, I was proud of my new nickname. It seemed like everyone else hid behind their given name and would not identify themselves as a Mutt. But not me. I was a Mutt and proud of it.

"Growing up, I was easy to remember. And as long as there were friends to meet, I was gladly introduced to them as Mutt. So as Mutts go, I was friends with everyone. Hey, I was lucky to be a Mutt. After all, you know how humans are sometimes. I learned of racism at an early age. It was so ugly to see name-calling.

"But I was a Mutt just like most of them. They just didn't want to admit it. Humans have been on earth a long time. They don't realize that they are all related to each other from some time in the ancestral past. It was impossible not to be, you know.

"But not me. I was the new Mutt and never experienced a problem anywhere with anyone. So my life and my understanding of my roots were pure and clear. I came from my past, and my past was from Everywhere, which we all know to be true. There were others who just could not comprehend, but the day will come when they do, as you know. Prejudice is a human thing and stupid, as we all learn sooner or later."

"True, oh so true," I say. "So tell me of your journey."

"Well, like I said, Jackie and I were best friends. I had two older brothers, three sisters, and then I, the Mutt, came as the last of the litter." He laughs. "Yes, there were six of us. My father was a baker. He made baked goods and had many employees at his bakery. You could smell the baking for quite some distance. It was really inviting, as I learned over the years. My mother was seamstress of sorts. Her primary responsibility was to take care of our family, of course, but she made the hats, coats, and aprons for my father's employees. She did from the beginning and just never stopped until she was too old to do so. Then my youngest sister took over the uniform making. My other two sisters delivered day-old breads and goodies to the local orphanages and shelters. They loved their chores. My father's company prided in our charity of giving. I sense we all worked for the bakery at some point or another. My two oldest brothers became bakers too. They helped to expand the bakery over time to include other locations.

"Our bakery was very successful. My father said, 'Everyone has to eat, you know.' And if his bakery could maintain its quality of goodness, then our family should not change but follow his footsteps.

"*Quality of goodness* was our bakery's motto and how our family lived and loved each other. Love thy neighbor is what we were taught when I was young and how we lived.

"My mother and father made it very clear to each of us how important it was for our family to set an example for our community. After all, the bakery is, in my father's opinion, the cornerstone of what each family should stand for. We were to provide the basics of life to everyone, not only baked goods but also who we are and how we live. This is the quality of goodness and what it meant to each of us.

"My father always had time for us, at home and at the bakery. He was busy, always, as was my mother, but he always, always had time for us and his employees too. He was the walking example of goodness. You know, you have had the same, as your Pap was just like my father. And, oh yes, we all love Pap too.

"With that, it's easy for you to understand my family. I grew up under the expansion of our bakery, as my older brothers picked up where my father left off. My father uncloaked late in life. He worked hard till the day he didn't. His uncloaking occurred at work, where I think he wanted to be that day. It was, as he wanted, to be a typical day at the bakery. And we kept our bakery baking through it all, just as he wanted.

"This verified the importance of quality of goodness, just like the values we followed. After all, aren't they really the same? Goodness is a good wrapper for the values. Every baked good from our bakery always had goodness in the ingredients. It was my father's way of passing along value to everyone.

"And that tradition held through my generation.

"I married twice. My first wife, Lisa, was my love of life. She and I were connected like my dreams come true. Sad to say, she became ill early on, and she uncloaked only to return to the Everywhere. Her journey was complete, as I believe her assignment was to teach me real love and what it meant. She was my soul mate.

"I was sad, but then I met Tenisha. She was a wonderful woman and partner. I loved her too but in a different way. She and I needed each other, I think. We were best friends, and that proved to be our assignment to each other. She was always there when I needed her. Sad to say, I did not have children with either of my wives. That I always regretted, but it was not to be.

"My nieces and nephews, however, kept me busy. I was to be their favorite uncle over time. Yes, we were all bakers. It was the quality of goodness that kept us going.

"My older brothers and two of my older sisters followed my parents over time and returned to the Everywhere. My last sister and I were to make sure our nieces, nephews, and her two children were to maintain the bakery and make sure goodness was on every wrapper, if you know what I mean. I think we did well, as they all learned and adjusted their lives to be bakers.

"But for some reason, it was not to be the same. Yes, they maintained the bakery over time. But I am not sure they ever took the time to teach their children of the importance of the bakery and the need for charity and goodness in it all. You see, after my sister and I returned to the Everywhere, we continued on with a few visits in our transition. It was as if the next generation had lost something. Their love for the bakery waned over time. I cannot understand why. Our quality of goodness was not the same, as it was not in their hearts to be bakers, I guess.

"As if a disease occurred, the power and greed overwhelmed them, and they sold our bakery to the highest bidder. The quality of goodness was gone. It came off the wrapper. The government would not permit it, as it was not a true ingredient.

"As you can see, our bakery was what has happened to many humans over the generations. The quality of goodness is gone from their hearts.

"They are all Mutts as before, but Mutts are to be loving and full of goodness. It's to be baked into their DNA, as I used to say. But now the quality of goodness is missing, and now the wave has returned with the biggest assignment of them all. Return the quality of goodness to the hearts and souls of humans. Teach family, love, honor, trust, and peace. Bring quality of goodness back to the wrappers in the bakery wherever it is not. It's an ingredient that must be included.

"So that's why my visit is with you today. I am here as a reminder of what life can be about. Look at the creek in front of you. Clear and pure and full of the quality of goodness. It's here and should be on earth too.

"Press forward with your assignment. It's just one of many of the assignments of the wave. But each ingredient is important, just as the values are to the survival of humans.

"So there you have it from one Mutt to another. Bring back the quality of goodness to the bakery. I know you can. It is an ingredient of everything good in life.

"May peace and love be with you. Turn up the ovens. Turn on the presses. There is a lot of printing and baking yet to do.

"And Ronald the Mutt is off to enjoy another day of goodness."

Pap's Message

Good morning to us all.

I open the portal today to a new view. As usual, however, there is a valley with two stumps perched in the foothills of the mountain behind me and a range on either side stretching as far as I can see. But there is a difference in the valley. There are fields and fields of crops as it appears. I recognize corn, wheat, and other grains.

A creek winds its way through the fields, and in the distance, it appears to be rice patties, as the water shimmers through from underneath.

It's very organized looking, but there are no beings tending the fields. There are hundreds of spirits about who seem to know their way around. They have specific directions they have chosen, as if they have been here before. And they most likely have many times.

However, I do sense that this is not earth. I cannot tell why, but this is just a bit different in its own way.

I do recognize one spirit coming my way. It's my Pap! I can recognize Pap from afar. He has this steady flow of movement, slow but full of grace.

Pap comes to me, and we greet each other with what feels like a hug.

However, I can best describe there is nothing but love all around us.

Pap says, "You look well." And he laughs.

I say, "What's so funny?"

He says, "Everyone looks great here, even when you are just visiting. It's like the law of the land here in the Everywhere. It's so perfect, even you look great." And we both laugh at his teasing.

He and I both have a seat and just enjoy the silence of the moment. I must say, my emotions are running high as I begin to tear up. I laugh at myself and say, "Sorry, Pap, but you know I miss you so. It's just really great to see you again."

Pap laughs as only he can and says, "I am never far away. In fact, I can be at your side in less time than you can imagine. After all, you are my project." He laughs. I join in with.

"I am sure you have your hands full," I say, and we both laugh.

I ask, "Pap, this is not earth, is it?"

Pap says, "No. No, it's not. But it sure is beautiful, isn't it? Just look at the perfect fields of crops. Have you ever seen such a sight?"

"Is there a significance to this sight for you?" I ask.

Pap says, "Well, yes, in a way. If you remember, I always thought the most beautiful view was a new field of young growth, Mother Nature at her best. Well, here—this is like my dream valley. Just look out over the horizon. Nothing but field after field of new growth."

And as he stops as if to listen, I can feel and hear rain beginning to fall. No clouds to speak of but rain just the same. It is soft and warm as it touches my skin. Pap says, "Remember, can you hear the corn growing? Its leaves are squeaking to eke out of its stock. I have always loved that sound." He sits there listening.

And then the rain lightens a bit to a soft drizzle.

"Wow," says Pap, "I can never get tired of this view. I come here not as often as I would like, but it's a treat every time."

"Besides this wonderful visit, what brings you here today? I know you have lots of responsibility here, as I am told by many."

Pap laughs. "I have no more than any other spirit, you know. It just seems that many look up to me for some reason. It's always amazed me, frankly."

I say, "But, Pap, that's how it was for you on earth. Remember? You did not say much, but you said a lot just by your actions and your love for everyone."

Pap looked at me with a surprised look. He said, "Well, that's how we are all supposed to be. I would like to think you learned that from me."

"I did, Pap. That's why I am here too. You have given me this great task. I am blessed by the assignment."

"Well, this view," Pap says, "you know, humans can have this view again on earth or some other planet. They just have to learn and live by the values again. It's really quite simple.

"Remember when you were young, and we were all on our farm? When it rained like this and we were on the porch, we could hear the corn growing, and we all sat there and just enjoyed Mother Nature at her best. Well, we were just poor farmers, as you know, but we were rich in love and values. That's all we had, and as you have learned, that's all we needed. Life was perfect then, even on earth. I remember those days vividly, as if they just happened yesterday.

"All humans have those moments, you know. Every human has their own private time when they can reason and think through life's lessons. That special time for each when no others are around, and you are only inside your own thoughts. That's when humans can return to the reality of the messages of the Everywhere—if each human could remember how they got where they are at that specific moment in time, how all they brought with them was their spirit and the values, and that life was no more necessary than that moment. The earth would be so much better. Don't you think?

"So it's up to you to teach each one you touch to find that moment and reflect on their past when they started their journey. That is the answer to the reality of the Everywhere. That is when humans can learn of their roots to life as it truly is. It's like sitting here looking out over these perfect fields in this perfect valley with these perfect mountains hugging life. It's everywhere around you here.

"Well, that can be the same on earth too. It was once. Remember?"

I say, "Pap, I think of it often. I remember getting up in the morning, taking my pony, Nellie, and Major, our dog, for a walk to the meadow. We used to sit under a tree there and just watch the clouds go by and listen to the sounds of nature. I had those perfect moments often when I was young and innocent."

"Exactly," Pap says. "No reason you can't have those moments now. No reason others can't have those moments now. Each human has those special times almost every day. You must teach them again to remember those times and learn from them. The Everywhere is just around the corner from those moments, you know.

"Perfection is on the other side of the veil or the dimension. It is there for everyone. That is the reality of the moment each and every day. When humans can learn how easy this is and how values keep their lives steady with lessons of learning and love, the earth becomes a better place almost immediately.

"As you know, there is a lot going on with the population explosion and all. Humans really have only one choice, and yet they think they have more. But the reality of the Everywhere makes the choice simple. It's all about family, love, honor, trust, and peace. Just as simple as that. These values are in each and every human, just waiting for the moment to reappear. And it can happen today or tomorrow for each. All they have to do is take that private moment and focus on how they got to earth and where they will return. After all, the Everywhere, well, is everywhere, just like here.

"These perfect fields await everyone. Enjoy your journey. That's what you must teach. Your journey started out pure and perfect, and that's how it will end. So enjoy the time you have on your journey, and each journey becomes more perfect when you do.

"Your assignment seems so monumentally large, I am sure. Everywhere you look, humans have forgotten their roots, so to speak. They have overlooked their own reality and have permitted greed and power to control their actions and thoughts.

"Fear is everywhere. Fear of the unknown is the most fearful fear of all.

"You being afraid of heights, well, that fear is different. You got that from me." He laughs. "But fear of the unknown is the worst. And yet each human really knows the unknown. They just have to take that private time each day and focus on the reality of the moment, and the Everywhere, the perfection of the Everywhere, will peek through the veil of the journey.

"It's just that simple. So make sure you speak of this in your travels as you meet new friends. Today is a gift to you from me. This is your clarification, so you can enjoy your journey too, knowing now how simple it is to teach all."

Pap moves from the stump as I stand. We both hug as when he held me as a newborn. I have never felt so much love.

But then, in reality, I always felt that love from my Pap. We look at each other and need not say a word as he saunters slowly off to enjoy the perfection of the fields. After all, Pap is a farmer through and through and will always be. He loves nature and life and love. His life is perfect, as he says. Mine is too. I just need that moment each day like all others.

It's time to return and enjoy my journey too …